Photo: Nicholas Watt

Fred Hilmer AO has held a number of key leadership and governance roles. He was President and Vice Chancellor of the University of New South Wales from 2006 to 2015, having previously served as Chief Executive of John Fairfax Holdings from 1995 to 2005.

In the early 1990s, Fred chaired the National Competition Policy Review Committee, which lead to far-reaching reforms in competition policy. In 1991, he was awarded a special John Storey Medal from the Australian Institute of Management for his contribution to management thinking.

Fred's earlier roles included almost twenty years with McKinsey and Co., with Ten as Managing Partner (Australia), before co-founding Port Jackson Partners.

Fred left McKinsey in 1989 to take on the role of Dean and Director of the Australian Graduate School of Management. It was at this time he became heavily involved in corporate governance.

Fred served as a Director of TNT, Coca-Cola Amatil, Macquarie Bank; Chair of Pacific Power; and Deputy Chair of Foster's Brewing Group and Westfield Holdings Ltd and related companies.

He graduated in law from the University of Sydney and was awarded a fellowship to undertake further law studies at the University of Pennsylvania before winning a Joseph Wharton Fellowship and completing his MBA at the Wharton School of Finance in the late 1960s.

He published his first books, *When the Luck Runs Out* and *New Games, New Rules* in the 1980s, followed by *Strictly Boardroom: Improving governance to enhance company performance* (1993, 1998), *The Fairfax Experience: What the Management Texts Didn't Teach Me* (2007). He is the co-author of *Management Redeemed: The case against fads that harm management* (1998) and *Working Relations: A fresh start for Australian enterprises* (1993).

ISBN 9781761280214 (print)

Published in Australia and New Zealand by:

Brio Books, an imprint of Booktopia Group Ltd
Unit E1, 3-29 Birnie Avenue, Lidcombe, NSW 2141, Australia
briobooks.com.au

Printed and bound in Australia by Pegasus Media & Logistics

FSC® www.fsc.org MIX Paper from responsible sources FSC® C008194

The paper in this book is FSC® certified. FSC® promotes environmentally responsible, socially beneficial and economically viable management of the world's forests.

Proudly Printed In Australia

booktopia.com.au

Fred Hilmer

What's Wrong With Boards

Rethinking corporate governance

Fred Hilmer

brio
BOOKS

Contents

Acknowledgements

Books such as this don't just happen. Nor are they the result of any one person's efforts.

What inspired me and the team who worked on this book was that people we really respected believed there was a real need to re-examine governance in light of a cascade of governance failures.

The first thank you goes to those who we spoke to in the months prior to and while writing the book. Many of these early conversations were the product of some significant effort by John Connolly. Thank you John for this early push, as well as comments on various drafts.

Then comes the hard part – turning a set of ideas and incidents into clear and readable drafts which trigger the next round of writing.

This book was inspired by conversations with directors and colleagues. We thank those we spoke to in the months prior to and while we wrote this book. A particular vote of thanks for those within this group who read drafts and provided typically excellent feedback. Each of our reviewers devoted significant time and gave invaluable comments. Thank you to Woo Kim and Tim Willetts, AGSM MBA students, who conducted the extensive literature search that provided an early stimulus and sense check for our key ideas.

Thank you also to Felicity Hughes who contributed to our initial discussions and led some of the landmark research, and to Matthew Barrett who provided key analyses. Thanks also to Kristy Meers, Vanessa Nguyen and Roisin Heidenreich who helped keep us on track. And thanks to the late Linda Weir who could turn my appalling handwriting into typed text.

This book would not have been possible without numerous key contributions from Byron Pirola and Grant Mitchell. Byron, Grant and I have been colleagues in a number of endeavours over the years including consulting assignments and pro-bono advice to me in my role as President and Vice Chancellor of UNSW. Their focus and assistance in getting the book done as well as we were collectively able was critical.

Finally thanks to our agent, Jeanne Ryckmans, our publicist Debbie McInnes and our publisher, Jon MacDonald.

After extensive team discussions, I am pleased to say all who worked on the book agreed with its content. Consequently I have used 'we' and 'our' interchangably with 'I' and 'my'.

Preface

Why have we written this book?

The new director smiled inwardly as he entered the office tower on the way to attend his first Board meeting. The director had recently retired after a successful career in finance. Getting two or so directorships at major companies was, in his mind, a perfect way to keep active and give something back now full-time work was over.

As he approached the security desk an administrative assistant came up to him, welcomed him and handed him a security pass for future attendance at meetings in the building. He felt good about the directorship. Everyone he had been in contact with during the headhunting process had been polite, respectful and friendly. He also knew a few of the other directors, some quite well, having worked with them on tough deals in his previous roles. The director looked forward to being on the same side as his colleagues, working to build the business and generate respectable returns for the shareholders.

Unfortunately, the good feelings and optimism about the role didn't last. Compliance matters dominated the agenda. The volume of papers to read and digest was mind-numbing. Managers seemed to be looking over their shoulders at what regulators were signalling rather than at the markets in which the company competed. As a consequence, there never seemed enough time spent on the business issues facing the company and the strategy it was following. Moreover, while questions were treated politely, he wished he or some other colleagues would push harder and go deeper into what niggled him. Also, while the answers to questions from him and the other directors were ostensibly welcomed, he couldn't help feeling that managers thought most questions, and the answers given, added little to decisions the Board faced. Put more bluntly, there was a quiet undercurrent that characterised many questions as "dumb".

This bothered him, as while the company's performance was adequate, it had seen better days. Management believed that fine-tuning strategy, cutting costs and strengthening the balance sheet would restore profitability. More fundamental questions about the strategy were answered by off-the-cuff points of view from the CEO, often supported by the finance director. These questions were scheduled to be debated at the Board retreat, but PowerPoint dominated and little was decided.

Fast forward five years. While the company had become more efficient and managed its balance sheet well, sales growth was sluggish and market share was under pressure. Private equity firms were showing increasing interest and a takeover was on the cards.

While this is fiction, the issues it raises are not. The public company governed by an independent Board is under pressure. In our view flawed governance is the key issue. Almost all major decisions are and can only be made by the Board, including critical appointments (CEO, chair and directors), major investments and strategy. If these decisions are poorly made the buck stops with the Board.

We contend all is not well with governance not just in Australia but more widely, as failures here have parallels in most economies where public companies are significant players. Hence this book.

Our starting point is to reiterate the critical roles played by large publicly listed companies with widely held shares.

The governance of large public companies matters – really

matters. Large, publicly listed companies with widely held shares are a key element of market economies. These companies bring together the capital and talent needed to operate complex, large scale businesses, and can take risks that smaller firms cannot. Modern, well-functioning complex economies rely on the likes of large banks and other financial institutions, retail chains, resource companies, key infrastructure providers and major technology companies. These large publicly-listed companies also provide democratised investment access to smaller shareholders, allowing them to construct portfolios that reflect their preferences for returns and risk, and type of business they choose to be involved with. According to an ASX study in 2020, 6.6 million Australian adults or 35% of the population hold listed investments (excluding superannuation).

In an increasingly complex and rapidly evolving environment, these companies require strong and effective governance to serve their shareholders well. When things go awry in the large listed company world, it matters. Beyond an immediate impact on shareholder value, the consequences can damage trust in business as providers of essential services, and as investors of shareholder capital.

Consequently, when things do go wrong, the immediate call is "who's responsible?" and "why did they allow these undesirable outcomes to occur?". Too often, the answer is simply and unhelpfully: "poor governance".

The governance problems we now face appear to be sufficiently different to those of the past that we believe fresh thinking is required.

Without this fresh thinking, we believe governance in public companies will not only not improve, but is likely to further decline.

Our overarching concern is that the expectations being created and enforced by Australia's current approach to corporate governance are unreasonable given current governance practices: they require Boards to have a command of detail, often in highly technical specialised areas, as well as a clear "big picture" perspective. As a result, the Board may act in ways that may not improve outcomes, and consequently distract from more valuable activities. In other words, the current direction of travel of governance reforms is at great risk of making leadership quality, company performance and stakeholder outcomes worse over time.

Our focus is very much on how a Board is constituted, structured, managed and operated. It was put to us that we should also examine and critique the legal framework within which Boards work. There is also substantial evidence that Australian directors are more heavily regulated than in other jurisdictions. Based on research in conjunction with the law firm Freehills, former Australian Institute of Company Directors (AICD) chair John Colvin argues that:

> *"Directors are subject to too many criminal offences, and too many of those offences allow conviction on the basis of strict or positional liability without the ordinary protections of the criminal law."*[1]

Mr Colvin concludes:

> *"This approach is not reasonable and is out of step with the regulation of other professions and occupations within Australia and the regulation of directors in other similar jurisdictions."*

This is strong evidence that the issue of directors' liability is important and that reforms could help improve governance. That said, on reflection we decided not to focus on this issue for three reasons:

- First, company law is not our expertise. Our backgrounds are with improving the performance of companies through strategies and operating reforms.

- Second, company law and regulation should facilitate and encourage good performance; if not, the laws should be changed. However, appropriately addressing legal reform of this type would be a substantial publication in itself.
- Third, regulation of governance, in particular directors' liability, is a topic that evokes strong views. The ensuing debate would drown the discussion of improving governance.

Governance crises have a common pattern. There is usually an accumulation of specific problems, including unanticipated losses or fraudulent or unethical behaviour. Over time, a sense of an overarching brokenness appears. What follows are demands that something must be done, leading to the imposition of new rules and regulations with a declaration that this can never happen again. If only this were true.

In 1993, during one of these periods of perceived poor governance, I chaired the Sydney Institute's review of governance. The resulting book, *Strictly Boardroom*, argued that:[2]

> ***"[T]he key role of a Board should be to ensure that corporate management, properly taking account of risk, is continuously and effectively striving for above average performance. This was not to deny the Board's additional role with respect to shareholder protection."***

After analysing losses in major listed companies, the contributors concluded that poor business judgements in boom markets – paying too much or borrowing too much – rather than misconduct or inappropriate entrepreneurial behaviour, were the main causes of poor performance in the 1990s. The *Strictly Boardroom* group were concerned that the increasing focus on complying with regulation and consequential prescriptive governance practices were taking the Board and management's attention away from their main performance enhancing role.[3]

However, in the late 2010s and early 2020s, we saw a new type of governance crisis develop.

The poor behaviour and misconduct examined in *Strictly Boardroom* occurred in few companies, none of which was a leader in its industry. This time poor conduct is more widespread. Leading companies – major banks, insurance and wealth management companies, telcos and energy producers – have been accused of material governance failures. None have collapsed, but as more evidence of improper behaviour emerged the crisis reached into senior management ranks and the Board. For example, during 2019 and 2020 three of the four major banks and two leading wealth managers lost both their chairs and CEOs. It is questionable whether this would have happened without the scrutiny of the Royal Commission and other reviews of and by regulators.

Another difference has been the nature of the financial impacts of governance failures. Rather than causing major financial losses, in many cases the misconduct increased profit – at least in the short-term – at the expense of customers and employees.

Australia is not alone in facing these issues. Australian governance problems can be seen as part of an international governance challenge. As noted by former president of the Business Council of Australia, Graham Bradley, in his 2019 Bathurst lecture,[4] in 2015 the world's largest automobile manufacturer, Volkswagen, sold more than 10 million small diesel cars fitted with computer algorithms designed to defeat emissions testing required by US, European and other national environmental regulations. It was eventually revealed that this scandal went well beyond VW's engineering department and that very senior company officers were aware of the fraud, resulting in the resignation of the CEO, chairman and other senior executives, and ongoing criminal prosecution against some of them.

Similarly, a major scandal in 2017 engulfed Wells Fargo, the third largest US bank and an organisation that had survived the global financial crisis without major losses. At Wells Fargo, 5000 employees, including the chair and CEO, were fired for facilitating the opening of financial product accounts for customers without the customers' knowledge or consent. As well as massive fines, the US Federal Reserve Bank restricted the bank's growth while demanding the replacement of four Wells Fargo Board members, without any judicial finding of fault on their part.[5] The basis for this ruling was that the directors should be held accountable for poor oversight of the culture and operations of Wells Fargo. In the Federal Reserve Bank's view, the directors' "performance in addressing these problems is an example of ineffective oversight that is not consistent with the Federal Reserves' expectations for a firm of WFC's size and scope of operations". Ramifications of this episode continue, including a US$3 billion settlement with the US Justice Department in February 2020.[6]

A final difference this time relates to how governance issues are being identified and managed. Previously, a typical response to governance crises has been to create a committee of inquiry focussed on designing reforms to the process of governance. This type of response arguably began with the Cadbury Committee in the UK in 1992,[7] and for some time review committees have been the main response to a governance crisis.

Before Cadbury there was no code of desirable governance practices (and no shortage of improper conduct). The absence of a code was seen as a gap that should be filled, a task Cadbury and his committee tackled with support from the London stock exchange, the Financial Reporting Council and the accountancy profession. The committee developed a code of 'best practices' that companies were expected either to adopt or to explain to the shareholders why they had not done so. Cadbury's code was widely adopted including in Australia, where the code has evolved into the ASXs Corporate Governance

Principles. Reaction to Cadbury was generally positive, however my own view, set out in *Strictly Boardroom*, was that Cadbury over emphasised the conformance roles of the Board and under emphasised the Board's role in enhancing performance.

This time, governance matters have been more likely to be addressed by a judicial or regulatory agency than a body specifically investigating governance. Australia's financial services sector, for example, was the subject of an interlocking set of inquiries with a range of objectives – all of which made major and valuable findings about governance issues. A Royal Commission investigated the industry with a remit extending far beyond governance.[8] In parallel, the Australian Prudential Regulatory Authority (APRA) reviewed governance culture and accountability within the country's largest bank, CBA[9], finding its success had "dulled the senses of the institution", particularly in relation to the management of non-financial risks. Never had such a significant and respected institution been subject to such a review by a regulator, with recommendations going to the heart of how the organisation was directed, led and managed. Subsequently the capabilities of APRA itself became the subject of a Federal Government inquiry.[10] None of these inquiries were about governance per se, but each made substantial and typically very critical findings about major governance failings. More recently, a set of inquiries into Crown Casino have examined governance practices, but with a specific set of questions in mind, not a focus on governance itself.

The Financial Services Royal Commission findings reflect the distinctive aspects of this governance crisis. Unlike, for example, the Royal Commission into HIH insurance, this was not an investigation stimulated by a financial collapse.[11] Unlike 2000 and 2008, there had been no financial crisis or corporate collapses. There had not been Enron or Lehman Brothers type failures.

The Bergin inquiry into Crown Casino in New South Wales was established in 2021 to question the fitness of Crown to hold a gaming license. Governance issues were an important part of the inquiry's work and a number of themes emerged. These included ethical conduct, risk management and oversight, as well as board composition, including independence, and remuneration and incentives. The inquiry noted that scrutiny of governance has intensified due, in part, to extensive external reviews such as the banking Royal Commission. While there are obvious differences between banking, funds management and casinos, the relevant principles of good governance have much in common.

The issues this time were about ethics, compliance with the law, and community expectations about standards of behaviour. This new formulation encouraged recognition and examination of conduct that was not illegal but nevertheless unacceptable. It recognised a newly prominent strand of thinking about the objective of governance, including how Boards were being asked to balance the interests of shareholders, customers and the community at large.

The report also positioned governance issues not in a legal realm but in the realm of ethics, and of practical action. Commissioner Kenneth Hayne took the view that new laws were not needed. He concluded that six principles, all of which he emphasised were adequately covered by current laws, needed to be properly adopted by companies to address the issues identified through the Royal Commission he oversaw. The six principles are:[12]

1. Obey the law
2. Do not mislead or deceive
3. Be fair, especially with customers
4. Provide services that are fit for purpose

5. Deliver services with reasonable care and skill
6. When acting for another, always act in their best interest.

This approach suggested governance should be grounded on basic, fundamental principles and less on prescriptive rules.

As corporate Australia was coming to terms with the findings of the Royal Commission and reforms proposed by regulators, Covid-19 struck. No business has been exempt from its effects.

This is less a governance crisis and more an acute governance challenge. For many firms, survival became the overwhelming issue. For firms with viable businesses, protecting the safety of employees and customers, as well as adapting to major changes in how people and goods could move around, was an urgent and high-stakes challenge across entire organisations. Over time, firms began to define what a post Covid-19 world would look like for them and how the firm could best adapt or otherwise change its business model and practices. This could include, for example, technology-driven adaptations that accelerated and became embedded through the pandemic, such as working from home and an increased use of on-line shopping.

We observed changes in governance practices in response to this challenge. It became clear that the necessities of coping with Covid-19 were revealing how large publicly-owned companies adapted governance when the pressure was on. Boards reacted by establishing ad hoc committees, choosing how to involve directors with specialist skills in time critical decisions, and increasing the frequency – and heavily modifying the agendas – of Board meetings.

While the pandemic is still playing out, some key governance issues it has triggered remain unresolved, including:

- How should the Board scan the environment and decide on risks they will deal with before crisis strikes?

- How should the Board modify its priorities, activities and approach when crisis hits?
- What lessons have been learned after the crisis has passed and a new normal has emerged?
- Do we have the right people on Boards to make the contributions required to make critical decisions?
- How can leadership by the chair of the firm's governance approach be made more responsive to firm circumstances?
- Should a focus on critical decisions rather than standard processes be a norm that goes beyond times of crisis?

These unprecedented events should have stimulated new, more creative thinking about how governance approaches can address the fundamental concerns identified by Hayne, and that persist even as firms adapt to a post-Covid world.

The fundamental duty of a Board remains a challenging one. To quote from a paper by Kate Towey and Charles Ashton of the law firm Allens:[13]

> *"As the impact of the Covid-19 pandemic first emerged many Boards focussed on their organisation's response to the immediate crisis. Boards must now turn their minds towards recovery and not lose sight of their overarching role and responsibility for effective organisational governance, strategic direction and planning.*
>
> *As Board agendas become more cluttered it is easy for the performance side of governance to receive inadequate attention."*

This more innovative and substantive conversation has been slow to emerge. Instead, we have observed – and our interactions with senior directors and executives confirm – a lack of clarity about the fundamental governance problems that should be addressed. Consequently, many improvement suggestions made over recent years amount to amplifying current practices in the hope that more-of-the-same will improve governance and firm performance.

The combination of pressure to improve governance without a path to fundamental change meets a common response from directors. The tendency is to retreat into form over substance via box-ticking processes, all based on so-called best practices. Their intention is to protect themselves against accusations of failed governance when something inevitably goes wrong.

What's missing from this conversation are ways to strengthen the Board's role, to better equip directors to meet governance challenges.

This book has therefore been written to provoke a more fundamental and far-reaching conversation about governance than we have witnessed to date. It is intended as an aid to those who sit on the Boards of Australian publicly-listed companies, the executive teams who work with them, the advisers who support them, and the regulators who oversee their activities and performance. Its objective is to help large listed companies deliver on their potential as wealth creators and on the delivery of important products and services, and as a source of meaningful satisfying employment opportunities. Since completing the book, we have had feedback that the issues we discuss are also relevant to smaller, unlisted companies that use a board to provide effective governance.

The focus and intent of this book emerged from our experiences of working with and for those who are responsible for governing public companies. We observed broad dissatisfaction about the state of the debate and the thinking around governance. What started out as an informal conversation over a lunch moved onto a series of informal round-tables and then numerous one-on-one interviews with chairs, directors and experienced Board advisers, as well as an ever-deepening review of academic and practical literature. We are indebted to those who generously gave of their time through interviews and follow-up discussions.

Those we interviewed clearly cared deeply about the issues and were troubled by where we find ourselves. What was intended just to be research for our own professional interests was met with strong encouragement to "try to make a contribution" in a more formal way.

We recognise that the topic of governance generally, and specifically of large complex organisations, is not a simple matter.

We found little empirical research, and few systematic attempts to gather evidence about what actually works in governance. Our conclusion is that in many cases, best practice is closer to "desirable practice" or, worse, the latest fad. This makes even more surprising the tendency for these practices to be positioned not as minimum standards or broad guidance, but as compliance tasks.

In chess, there is no answer to "what is the best move?". The best move depends on the specific game and the specific opponent facing the player. Similarly, our approach to working towards improved governance has been to focus on the specific, persistent, and important governance challenges that have been at the heart of company collapses, dissatisfied shareholders and stakeholders, and fraudulent and other types of illegal behaviour. We have sought to recognise that solving these problems may mean more flexibility to find and adapt "best fit" approaches. We have resisted the temptation to pronounce on best practice without linking the answer to the specific challenges facing the Board at a particular moment in a company's life.

This approach has had implications for the focus and scope of the book. At times, this book will re-emphasise things that are perhaps obvious but lost in the current discourse. At times it will address contemporary practices which have little supporting empirical evidence, or have been twisted from their original design. Finally, at times we will propose alternative and perhaps unusual approaches we believe deserve considered investigation and debate. Even though we may be pushing against the grain of current governance thought, we think this is part of grappling with a worthy and unsolved problem.

This is a complex challenge. Australia's default public company governance model is now competing against strong and well-established alternatives such as private equity, direct investments by large pension funds and sovereign wealth funds. If it is to survive into the next century as a vibrant part of a sophisticated and dynamic market economy, it needs to become a more efficient and effective means of marshalling financial and human capital.

The risks of continuing on the current course are that public companies become ineffective models for capital formation and wealth creation, relegating them to the graveyard of competitive corporate life. The upside is that better governance has the potential to improve performance and so strengthen the public company model.

We hope our approach will be seen as pragmatic rather than evangelical, practical rather than theoretical, and thought provoking rather than prescriptive. Our goal is to clarify the nature of the problem, identify principles and actions that help, identify practices we consider unhelpful and potentially destructive, and propose possible solutions we believe are worthy of proper debate and exploration.

Overview

Our thesis in a nutshell

We aim to help those who sit on the Boards of Australian publicly listed companies, the executive teams who work with them and the advisers who support them.

Our goal is to clarify the nature of the problem, identifying and applying principles that demonstrate where current practices are unhelpful, and propose solutions that we believe are worthy of further proper debate and exploration.

Our argument, and the structure of this book, is in three parts.

Part I: The nature of the governance challenge

In Chapter One, we review the differences in power, time spent, available information and incentives between full-time managers and part-time non-executive directors. Although necessary in current governance models, and in some respects an appropriate division of labour and responsibility, this imbalance has important governance implications.

To better understand these implications, and to allow analysis of potential solutions, in Chapters Two and Three we argue that the history of governance breakdowns suggests four major sources of failure, each of which has the potential to bring down large and successful companies but which drift in and out of focus. We also argue that each category of failure will require different responses.

We describe two of these challenges (Chapter Two) as failures of performance. These are:

- the acceptance of marginal performance, or in other words the failure of Boards to generate long-term returns that meet investor requirements and community expectations; and
- "can-kicking", or a deliberate unwillingness to confront failures in an existing business model or strategy. In short, this governance error is the equivalent of ignoring a problem in the hope it will go away.

Two further governance issues are ethical and legal failures (Chapter Three). These are unethical conduct, including actions that may already be illegal, and deliberate concealment of bad outcomes. These failures are more readily acknowledged than failures of performance. Despite this extra attention, we argue that these two failures are also persistent, and are very difficult to address within current governance structures and practices, particularly when directors who have concerns prefer to leave the Board rather than follow through on them.

Part II: More-of-the-same won't work

Our analyses and interviews have led us to conclude that the current approaches to improving governance, which we characterise as more-of-the-same, requires a fundamental rethink, not fine tuning.

We develop this case in Chapters Four and Five.

In Chapter Four, we argue that the four major governance failures persist because most governance reform ideas amount to more-of-the-same. We argue these reforms build from supposed best practice to add more constraints to the way Boards are constructed and operate. Specific more-of-the-same reforms have been accompanied by a transition from governance guidelines towards being prescriptive norms. This has limited the scope for innovation, including innovation targeted at specific governance problems.

This direction of travel has two linked problems. First, there is no evidence to support many elements of current so-called best practice reforms. This means evidence for the efficacy of more-of-the-same governance reform is missing. This is of particular concern, because as best practice guidelines move closer to prescriptive norms, failure to follow best practice is increasingly risky for Boards. This failure readily attracts disapproval of shareholders and proxy advisers, many of whom value compliance over effectiveness.

Second, the major elements of more-of-the-same add work for Boards without targeting improved outcomes. There are few efforts among governance experts to explicitly match reforms to the major governance problems. It also appears illogical to impose a uniform approach given the variety of situations Boards face. The resultant focus on process over substance prevents Boards and reformers from coming to grips with the hard issues. It encourages the appearance of good governance but not necessarily its achievement.

In Chapter Five, we illustrate the problems with more-of-the-same by reviewing the major elements of more-of-the-same governance:

- A heightened focus on director independence defined not by governance quality but by mechanistic standards;
- Director selection based on increasingly precisely defined technical competencies as described in a skills matrix and away from judgement based on experience;
- Increased disclosure of information to and by the Board that blurs accountability and reduces information quality; and
- Additional roles for the Board, only some of which are likely to improve outcomes.

We analyse each of these elements, and explain why logic and experience suggest these elements will not address the four major governance failures that concern us. We also describe a second problem: that more-of-the-same is unlikely to drive meaningful change that requires a departure from current practices.

This approach may be appropriate to set minimum standards, but it is unlikely to systematically improve outcomes – surely the most appropriate target of a best practice framework.

Part III: Equipping Boards to meet governance challenges

In Chapter Six, we argue that rather than focus on so-called best practice, Boards should focus on "best fit". The notion of best fit comes from contingency theory, the essence of which is captured simply by US sociologist William Scott, who specialises in institutional theory and organisation science:

> *"The best way to organise depends on the nature of the environment to which the organisation must relate."*[14]

We provide a framework to consider alternative governance models, and five specific governance structures are outlined and discussed. We don't advocate a "best" model. Rather we urge Boards to adopt, with shareholder consideration and approval, what best fits. This is a significant shift in mindset, and could lead to an appropriate divergence of governance models depending on a company's situation.

Discovering and implementing best fit is only part of the story about how to improve governance. Having a Board spend more time on additional prescribed issues or new areas of concern is not the answer. This has a real risk of blurring the lines between board and management, and so introducing a new governance risk. In Chapter Seven, we propose that Boards should give more focus to that which only a Board can decide, delegating other matters to executive leadership or Board committees.

In Chapter Eight, we argue for the elevation of the role of the chair in the quest for improved governance. As in most areas of economic activity, effective leadership is what distinguishes the best performers from the also-rans. Achieving best fit and appropriate focus depends critically on the leadership provided by the Board chair. In our interviews it was suggested that if only one change in governance was possible, that change should be to clarify the role and improve the functioning of the chair. We describe in Chapter Eight how this can be done.

* * *

Journalist and essayist H. L. Mencken wrote: "There is always a well-known solution to every human problem that is neat, plausible and wrong."[15]

The more-of-the-same approach to governance is simple, convenient, and supported by many in the governance industry. Its only problem is that it has not, and most likely will not, help directors and managers address fundamental governance issues.

Making progress means giving Boards the flexibility and the permission to adapt their approaches, allowing them to do their best in their specific circumstances.

PART I

The nature of the governance challenge

In Chapters One through Three, as we analyse the differences in power, time spent, information availability and incentives between full-time managers and part-time non-executive directors, we identify the governance implications that arise from these imbalances.

We argue that the history of governance breakdowns suggests four major sources of failure – each of which has the potential to bring down large and successful companies, but which drift in and out of focus. We also argue that each category of failure requires distinct responses.

We describe two of these challenges as failures of performance: the acceptance of marginal performance (failure to generate long-term returns that meet investor requirements and community expectations), and "can-kicking" (a deliberate unwillingness to confront fundamental failures in an existing business model or strategy).

We describe the other two types of governance failures as ethical and legal failures.

Chapter One

The governance problem

When a governance crisis breaks, the first question asked is "who is responsible?" followed by "how did they let this happen?".

In listed companies, the governance buck stops with the Board of Directors. This is where the ultimate power to make all key corporate decisions resides. Only the Board can hire and fire the CEO and chair. Only the Board can set incentive size and structures for the CEO, along with senior executive remuneration, and the remuneration approach more generally. Only the Board can approve major new investments or entering into new fields. The Board is central to discussions on capital raising and restructuring, alongside shareholders. And finally, Boards must oversee the core processes to ensure the Board and therefore shareholders are properly informed on matters of materiality, and that key risks are understood and managed.

The Board has these powers because it represents the owners of the firm. However, the essence of the governance problem is that the owners' interests are not always the same as managements'. In Corporate Governance Matters, Stanford Graduate School of Business professors David Larcker and Brian Tayan define corporate governance as a "collection of control mechanisms an organisation adopts to prevent or dissuade potentially self-interested managers from engaging in activities detrimental to the welfare of shareholders and stakeholders".[16]

Current corporate governance is often dated to *The Modern Corporation and Private Property*, written by Columbia Law School Professor Adolf Berle and Harvard University economist Gardiner Means in 1933. This work begins with a recognition of the new challenges posed by the growth in size and importance of the "modern giant corporation"[17] and the widening gap between ownership and control.

The potential for divergent interests extends beyond obvious conflicts of interest[18] in areas that are more complex but could also be more vital to a firm's success. These include:

- managers seeking to maximise their remuneration while Boards want to pay only a competitive package;
- management preferring soft targets in budgeting and incentive setting, while the Board wants realistic stretch targets;
- managers preferring to leave their employment at a time of their choosing, while Boards want to remove managers when they are not performing or have lost the confidence of the Board; and
- management pursuing acquisitions that make the firm larger, with a flow on to remuneration and more opportunities for managers, while effective Boards care less about company size and more about sustainable returns to shareholders.

Managing these divergent interests is never easy. The major decisions described above rely on complex financial and other analyses. Even apparently precise valuation calculations hide multiple judgements that require careful interpretation.

In these complex areas, providing sufficient oversight to navigate these divergent interests is challenging. We recollect a talk by David Beatty of the Rotman School of Management in Canada describing

"250 plays 3000". His point is that a non-executive director spends about 250 hours per year (roughly 2 to 3 days a month for 10 months) on preparing for and attending meetings. In contrast, management spends more like 3000 hours on what are usually 24/7 roles. Non-executive directors also have other interests, often a primary interest such as a CEO or chair position in another firm. Hence, unlike management roles, non-executive Board roles and the issues that come with them are not always front of mind.[19]

This time differential often creates a large imbalance in understanding the issues facing the company and the realistic options that may be available. And the imbalance gets worse as complexity of the governance task increases, due both to expansion in scope and scale of the business over time, and also the increasing expectations and obligations placed on Boards in terms of their role and conduct.

Growth in business size and complexity continues. Since *Strictly Boardroom* was published in 1992, the average market capitalisation of an ASX200 company has increased from A$3 billion to A$12 billion.

More important than value is operational size and complexity. For example, from 1992 to 2021 the Big 4 Australian retail banks grew from total revenues of A$40 billion to A$130 billion.

These firms are also operating new, more complex business systems. Technology has reconstructed every aspect of the firm's operations and risk management. Marketing has been transformed by social media; cost structures must embrace technology; strategy has to accommodate the ever-increasing number of potential disruptors. These are only some of the contemporary challenges that demand Board and management attention.

The mismatch between the demands created by business complexity and the capacity of typical Boards continues to increase. Our experience suggests that business complexity will continue to grow. Few of the contemporary challenges described above will disappear. In addition, more complex markets and customer preferences imply strategies with multiple levels, and place more emphasis on having compelling strategic initiatives across multiple horizons. More recently, awareness of the shortcomings of traditional large firm management structures has led to the evolution of new organisational forms, moving away from command and control approaches that (for all their weaknesses) have at least been straightforward to organise around and report on.

Increased business complexity amplifies a second mismatch between management and Board: the ability to accrue the right information, and crucially to direct self-discovery of information about key issues. Boards largely rely on documents provided by management often accompanied by verbal, off the cuff explanations to hold management to account. The job of the Board then entails making a judgement about the quality, accuracy and salience of the information being provided. At this point discussion can go off the rails and the leadership role of the chair becomes critical, a subject dealt with more fully in Chapter Eight.

To meet this challenge more effectively Boards are, as described to us in our interviews and through our own observations, being invited to become more focussed and to broaden their scope. This direction is despite a designed-in mismatch in information and time. This situation seems untenable.

Another way of understanding the governance task is to describe and unpick the most important categories of governance failures.

Our experience and interviews suggest directors might readily agree that managing divergent interests is a sensible description of their role. However, as a pragmatic guide to their activities, thinking about specific categories of governance failure can be more helpful. Identifying these categories helps provide a common language to address governance challenges.

Whether and how well governance reform proposals meet the governance challenges is a useful test against which calls for changes to governance practices can then be assessed.

There are two major categories of governance failures, each of which has two primary varieties as set out in Exhibit 1.

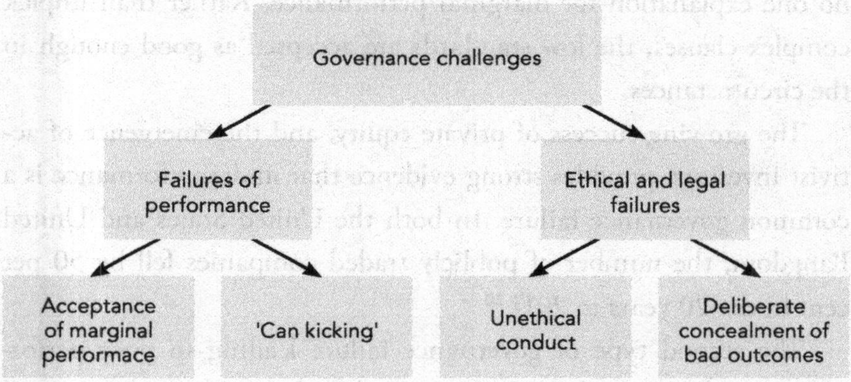

Exhibit 1

The first category is failures of corporate performance. The second is unethical and at times illegal conduct.

The first category includes the most common type of governance failure: the Board's acceptance of marginal performance by management. By marginal performance we mean achieving results that are just acceptable, but in the Board's view could be considerably better.

No one disputes that providing oversight of performance is a basic Board role. But what is meant by "good performance" varies widely. Is earning the cost of capital good performance? Is taking short-term pain for longer-term gain good performance? Is meeting the best practice guidelines of the relevant stock exchange good performance?

When is trading off stakeholder interests and economic returns good performance? To what extent is lack of innovation a measurable, valuable and forward looking performance test? And how should a Board act if faced with marginal performance?

Strictly Boardroom provided one possible answer to these questions – good performance was consistently being in the top half of relevant competitors on key performance measures. There is generally no one explanation for marginal performance. Rather than unpick complex clauses, the low standards are accepted as good enough in the circumstances.

The growing success of private equity, and the emergence of activist investors, provides strong evidence that underperformance is a common governance failure. In both the United States and United Kingdom, the number of publicly traded companies fell by 50 per cent in the 20 years to 2017.[20]

The second type of governance failure leading to poor performance is what we call can-kicking. Rather than pick up the can and deal with why it is on the road, the can is kicked ahead, in the hope that by the time the kicker reaches the can again the problem will go away, or it will become somebody else's problem to resolve.

In can-kicking, a Board chooses to live with specific performance issues or strategic problems rather than facing and addressing them. In our view can-kicking is a distinct and widespread case of accepting marginal performance. It can manifest as new business models emerge to attack current businesses, such as the migration of classified advertising from newspapers to the internet, or the increase in online retailing at the expense of bricks and mortar outlets, or discounting for new customers while creating a loyalty tax on existing customers.

The second category of governance failure is unethical and deceptive conduct. Evidence to the Hayne Royal Commission and its final report included examples of unethical conduct within large organisations that were expected to be compliant with best practice governance standards. Some examples concerned complex products where customers are not equipped to understand what is being sold, and when the salesperson takes advantage of the customer's poor understanding. Others included products designed or maintained to disadvantage customers. Beyond the financial services sectors, other regulatory reviews, as well as reviews of governance itself, suggest poor ethical standards are more widespread than most of the public, shareholders and directors believe to be the case.

Finally, deliberate concealment from the Board of actual or emerging problems is the rarest, but perhaps most difficult to navigate of the governance failures. This failure invites examination of the value of internal and external audits, but also whether the cost of these failures is sufficiently high to require changes to the way in which Boards receive and investigate information.

The following two chapters explore each of these failures in turn.

Chapter Two

Failures of performance

Major governance failures include issues of performance. Of course, Boards are accountable for preventing poor conduct. But of equal importance is the delivery of the type of superior business performance that leads to enduring institutions, capable of delivering positive outcomes for investors, customers, employees and communities.

Acceptance of marginal performance

A director we spoke to recalled a conversation with Board colleagues about their CEO's performance and succession.

These colleagues agreed the current CEO was "good enough" but clearly not outstanding; results were lacklustre and the executive team were not performing to their potential. Almost certainly, the Board would have been able to secure a CEO who would be a stronger performer, and with a greater chance of delivering improved business performance. But the challenge of going through a time-consuming selection process was, for a number of directors, too high a price to pay for an uncertain chance of attracting a better CEO.

Dealing with a CEO and top executive team who are modest but not top tier performers is one of the most challenging situations Boards face. Judgements about marginal executive performance require Boards to get underneath the top and bottom line results and form a view about whether management aspirations and expectations line up with those of the Board, often with input from large shareholders and analysts. Does the firm have a "big, hairy, audacious goal", to quote Stanford academic Jim Collins in *Built to Last*?[21] Are executives excited about their work and the challenges they face? Is the management team living off past successes, a view expressed in the 2018 APRA review of culture in the Commonwealth Bank,[22] or have they identified and begun to deliver on an ambitious agenda?

The governance challenge to consistently strive for excellence, not settling for the merely acceptable, is often overlooked. *Strictly Boardroom* recognised this challenge. At that time:[23]

> *"[E]xcessive concern with entrepreneurial misconduct [had] concealed a far more important and fundamental underlying concern: the continuing poor performance of many large firms in highly competitive markets."*

As described above, governance failures have now moved beyond "cowboy entrepreneurs" (in the bad sense) but the performance challenge remains – one that relates not only to poor firm performance but the creation and persistence of unsustainable business strategies that seek short-term gains at the expense of customers and stakeholders rather than long-term competitiveness through productivity and innovation.

Assessing performance

The meaning of performance is an increasingly important subject of Board dialogue.

To examine how successfully Boards have driven performance depends on understanding how it has been defined in the past, with consideration of how this may change in the future.

For the past several decades, Boards and senior executives have typically measured performance through the lens of shareholder returns:

- Shareholder returns and related financial metrics drive incentive structures, particularly long-term incentive structures, of listed firms. Many of these incentive structures also include achievement of strategic or operational metrics that in themselves are drivers of financial performance. For example, production targets, completion of major projects, or achievement of customer satisfaction metrics.
- Critical boardroom conversations have been conditioned on shareholder returns. Many strategic reviews begin with the examination of relative share price or total shareholder return performance. Setting targets associated with these metrics is a common top down process to help evaluate or compare strategies developed bottom up.
- Returns on shareholder capital have also been central to capital allocation decisions. Many firms recognise investor return expectations when setting hurdle rates or discount rates used in the modelling and assessment of major new investments.

Many firms are considering how they will define and measure performance in the future. This issue is dealt with in more detail in Chapter Four, but clearly the ability of a firm to define and deliver on a meaningful purpose – including but explicitly beyond returns to its investors – is an increasingly important definition of performance.

Even in this broadened definition of performance, returns for investors will remain an important benchmark for listed companies. The market for corporate control is as active as it has ever been. Some of this activity may be from cyclically low costs of capital, or from innovations such as special purpose acquisition companies (SPACs).

Tailwinds from the influx of interest in private markets, including private equity, unlisted infrastructure vehicles and pension funds looking to own assets directly, are likely to be more permanent. Finally, there is an increasing link between superior purposes, meaningfully executed, and future returns to investors – in other words, returns to investors will reflect the benefits of a more effective and appropriate purpose.

How prevalent is marginal performance?

To help identify marginal performance, we analysed the track record of ASX200 firms over the decade to FY2019. (We excluded FY2020 and FY2021 to exclude the impacts of Covid.)

We collected financial data from the 147 companies that were listed in the ASX200 across the entire decade. For each firm, for each year, we compared each company's net operating profit after tax with the annual cost of providing the capital employed. This cost was itself the product of total capital employed by the annual return – in per cent investors would expect. This cost, the weighted average cost of capital, was calculated by weighting the current cost of debt and cost of equity by the market value of each. The cost of equity was estimated by the risk free rate, the Bloomberg adjusted beta for each stock and a 6 per cent market risk premium, consistent with a range of contemporary estimates.[24]

Adding the annual figures gave a picture of excess returns above investor expectations across the decade. This analysis suggests few firms have outperformed their investors' expected returns, and marginal performance is the most common result.

Over the decade to FY2019:

- 51 firms, about 13 per cent of invested capital, delivered returns 1 per cent less than their Weighted Average Cost of Capital (WACC), or worse;

- 68 firms, about 49 per cent of invested capital, delivered returns 1 per cent or more above their WACC or better; and
- 28 firms, about 38 per cent of invested capital, delivered returns at their WACC +/- 1 per cent.

This analysis suggests there is plenty of marginal performance in our leading companies. Even though meeting the weighted average cost of capital should keep investors satisfied in theory, for a director in the ASX200 these findings should raise a suspicion that many management teams have been allowed to see investor expectations as a target, not a floor on acceptable performance.

Some but by no means all of these outcomes can be attributed to industry sector. Applying 10 common industry classifications shows the median firm has not met investor expectations in five sectors: utilities, metals and mining, oil and gas, real estate and industrials. In five others – banks, consumer discretionary, consumer staples, non-bank financials and health care – the median firm has met this hurdle. But in all sectors both outperformance and underperformance is present. Industry sector is a factor, but not an excuse, for failing to meet the challenge of marginal performance.

A third test is to understand the effectiveness of capital investment decisions made over the decade. The strongest firms can add to invested capital while increasing returns to shareholders. Only about a quarter of companies achieved this in the decade to FY2019; the remaining three quarters have seen excess returns decline, failed to find more attractive investment opportunities, or suffered from both problems.

This Australian analysis is backed by global research that suggests public firm performance is frequently modest, with fewer firms delivering strong shareholder outcomes. For example, in 2018 World Bank research[25] found that in 2015 the return on invested capital of the top decile of US listed firms was around 3.5 times the median; in 1995 this ratio was around three times, and in 1985 2.5 times.[26] These changes were driven by improved returns of the best firms, and also by the emergence of hi-tech platforms that have less need than traditional companies for invested capital.

A newer performance challenge is the emergence of alternative capital models. Activist investors, private equity investors, and investment or mutual funds are all increasingly willing to exert influence, including taking or keeping businesses out of the publicly listed sector if they believe it is a path to higher returns. Relying on the expectations of investors in public markets may no longer be a guide to acceptable returns. At the time of writing Sydney Airport, one of Australia's largest public companies, was taken over by infrastructure investors.

Poor shareholder performance creates other governance challenges

As well as disappointing shareholders, failure to adequately consider performance challenges can exacerbate or even cause other governance challenges.

Companies under performance pressure do not inevitably reach for unethical solutions to performance problems. Yet weaker performance does sharpen the choices before businesses, and these choices may begin to include some directions that may appear to jump start performance, but over time will do the opposite. In our experience this includes, for example, poorly designed cost reduction programs, aggressive accounting or radical strategic shifts that amount to change for change's sake. Being "seen to be doing something" can be easier than working out the much broader question of what changes will make a real difference. This performance pressure can also cross into other governance failures, including an increase in the tendency for management teams not to disclose areas of poor performance.

Acceptance of poor performance also includes the persistence of strategies that although attractive in the short term, are ultimately unsustainable. This class of strategies includes those that seek to enhance business financial performance through exploiting market failures, or information asymmetries, often at the expense of customers. Evidence to the Financial Services Royal Commission in particular highlighted the undesirable nature of this type of strategy.

To be clear, this is not a criticism of approaches that strike the best possible balance between customer needs and a firm's economics. It is, however, a challenge to Boards that adopt strategies to create advantage over their customers, instead of devising strategies that create advantage over current and potential competitors.

The flaws in this type of approach have begun to be exposed in two ways.

First, policymakers and regulators have sought to identify and examine business models that they see as unreasonably biased against customers' interests. For example, major inquiries into electricity and banking by the Australian Competition and Consumer Commission (ACCC)[27] and the Productivity Commission[28] have examined these industries from a consumer protection point of view – a broader remit than even the Financial Services Royal Commission. Particular attention has been paid to business models where quasi-compulsory purchases have been sold through unnecessarily complex or opaque pricing structures: electricity, insurance and some financial services products.

The result of these inquiries has been to extend new regulations and policies into product design and pricing, looking to protect customer interests in the absence of appropriate corporate conduct. In private health insurance, for example, the Federal Government became sufficiently concerned at the difficulty consumers faced in comparing products that in 2018 standard tiers of hospital products were introduced.

Second, new competitors are exposing these strategic flaws. At times, but not always, this has been made easier by customer scrutiny provoked by regulators. But it has been powerful, nevertheless. In superannuation, for example, customers have begun to switch towards many of the funds described as superior by a Productivity Commission report. This change in customer behaviour has no doubt been assisted by the Financial Services Royal Commission: funds receiving high inflows are rarely vertically integrated fund managers with potentially conflicted distribution models.

In addition, new digital businesses, with lower cost structures and the flexibility to try new approaches, are more easily able to make superior offers. In other cases, these new firms are seeking to design out features of traditional models that place the interests of the company and the customer into conflict, creating superior propositions for customers. In short, these businesses represent a new form of disruption, focussed on values and alignment of interests within traditional business models.

It is very difficult to arrive at and execute strategies that confer and maintain genuine sustainable competitive advantage. But businesses that achieve this are under less pressure to resort to unethical or unsustainable conduct to achieve strong performance, and so generate a powerful virtuous circle of positive reinforcing attributes.

Why does marginal performance persist?

The performance analyses above are available to every Australian director. They rely only on public data, and while the situation of every company differs, and the specific cause of high quality performance challenges may vary, it seems there are many firms where performance conversations are not occurring. The most likely explanation for this is that the conversations required are challenging and – unless framed correctly and conducted with the right incentives – unlikely to occur. There are at least three reasons for this:

- Arguments for dealing with marginal performance immediately are weak, contributing to problem avoidance. There is no burning platform, meaning it is easier to live with marginal performance than seek to improve significantly.
- Performance conversations, especially those dealing with difficult issues, are easy to swamp with process discussions.
- Some actions that are required to deal with marginal performance are risky and challenging to execute, and there can be perceptions that if they don't work key executives may be removed, or will move to less challenging environments.

As well as allowing the persistence of poor performance, these circumstances may also encourage a related but perhaps even more serious challenge we term can-kicking.

Can-kicking and the Board's role

Opportunities for Boards to address performance – particularly persistent performance issues – are increasingly rare. Directors we spoke to, and our own experience creating conversations about performance among Boards and senior directors, suggest conformance matters are crowding out performance discussions from Board agendas more than ever.

This environment, created and amplified by the governance failures we described above, is an especially poor match for a perceived shortening in investor time horizons, and a closely related shortening in CEO and senior management tenure. It also leaves little time for striking the right balance between performance and culture, including striking the balance between incentives that drive long-term returns and those that encourage improper behaviour.

The major risk is that lack of time, coupled with increasingly short-term objectives, give Boards a reason to avoid discovering and debating paths of actions that would lead, over time, to an unsustainable position.

In Predictable Surprises,[29] Harvard Business School Professors Max Bazerman and Michael Watkins[30] analyse "disasters we should have seen coming", including pandemics, weather extremes and rogue employees. These case studies, and others, led Bazerman and Watkins to suggest predictable surprises have the following characteristics:

1. Leaders knew a problem existed and the problem would not solve itself.
2. Organisation members recognise that a problem is getting worse over time.
3. Fixing the problem will incur significant costs in the present, while the benefits of action would be delayed.
4. Addressing the problem requires incurring a certain cost, while the reward is avoiding a cost that is uncertain but likely to be much larger.
5. Fixing the problem means moving away from a tendency to prefer the status quo – even when this is no longer sustainable.
6. Finally, there is a small vocal minority which benefits from inaction.

Our own experience is that many important strategic business challenges meet some of these criteria, and some all six. These characteristics also reveal why the typical solution – to "kick the can" down the road for someone else to deal with – is so attractive.

For listed firms, capital market valuations also provide an additional temptation for can-kicking. A willing coalition between Boards, investors and managers may prefer to believe a story rather than face an embarrassing about-face and reconstruction. Like the boiling frog, the temptation is to keep coping rather than plan for the inevitable comeuppance.

The result of these circumstances is that it often takes bold internal intervention or, more often, outside scrutiny to bring can-kicking to an end. Two examples illustrate these forces at work.

ABC Learning Centres

A private operator of child care centres, ABC Learning Centres, was part of a new approach in a sector that had previously been associated with not-for-profit or community-based operations.

ABC Learning Centres was founded by Eddie and Le Neve Groves. The attraction of the child care sector to entrepreneurs was obvious: it offered a combination of payment in advance, substantial government subsidies, and rising prices for centre properties. In 2002, Eddie Groves was reported to consider the business recession-proof.[31.]

ABC Learning grew rapidly, from 43 premises in 2001 to more than 1000 in 2008 – excluding a network of other centres overseas. This growth was applauded by the capital markets. ABC Learning shares rose rapidly. By late 2001 ABC shares were already around $14, a substantial increase from their $2 listing price.

However, by 2008 the firm had collapsed, and questions were being raised about what a Commonwealth Senate Inquiry[32] called "highly questionable business practices". According to the Inquiry, some of these practices related to the way in which ABC Learning conducted itself in the market. Some concerning aspects of conduct related to the quality of provision of care as well as actions towards other child care operators – ABC Learning's competitors.

But another variety of questionable practices led more directly to ABC Learning Centres' collapse. These relate to judgements by the Board and its auditors about the value of the business' intangible assets and the role of these intangible assets in driving reported profits.

Intangible assets were important to ABC Learning's financial position. Around the time of its collapse, about 80 per cent of total assets were intangibles. This included childcare operating licences that could not be traded and whose value came under substantial scrutiny.

Why does this constitute a can-kicking governance failure?

First, the value of intangible assets was the result of judgements of the ABC Learning Centres management, Board, and its auditors. In the case of the operating licences, the Inquiry found these assets did not have a readily identifiable market value. In the case of goodwill associated with acquisitions, this too was a product of ABC Learning's willingness to pay for acquiring other childcare operators. Sustaining these valuations, which clearly had questionable aspects, effectively kicked the can down the road until the next valuation event.

Second, an important effect of growth in intangible assets was a lack of focus on problems in the underlying business. The extent of these problems is revealed in the size of the rescue program following ABC Learning's collapse: temporary funding guarantees were needed to keep open about 660 of ABC Learning's Australian centres.[33] At the time of the collapse, around a quarter of ABC Learning's centres were unprofitable.[34]

External scrutiny from investors and the business press was important in bringing the can-kicking to an end. With the benefit of hindsight, the problems underlying ABC Learning were obvious and should have been dealt with much earlier. In a submission to the Inquiry, the new management of a post-collapse ABC Learning wrote:

"[U]nfortunately, the accounting practices that underpinned [the firm's] growth strategy appear to have served to materially inflate the true underlying operating performance of the business which is at the core of the problem. The public reporting of ABC's profitability gave rise to the perception that the provision of childcare was an extremely lucrative and profitable industry. This attracted significant investment and enabled ABC to accelerate its expansion plans, including forays into international markets."[35]

Can-kicking is ultimately about standards Boards set for themselves, in relation to compliance with the law, accounting standards or audit sign-offs. For example, ABC Learning was the subject of an extensive investigation by ASIC, including a five-year period of action on criminal charges against executives and a director, leading to one conviction. However, these actions concerned misleading conduct about related party transactions, not decisions with regard to the valuations of intangible assets or general business practices. Indeed, ASIC found that revaluations of operating licences were consistent with accounting standards, and the conduct condemned by subsequent management teams was, at the time, consistent with legal and accounting standards. This highlights the difficulties and challenges boards face, and therefore the importance placed on dealing with potential can-kicking.

WeWork

The We Company's August 2019 prospectus describes the company's mission as:

"[T]o create a world where people work to make a life, not just a living. We believed that if we created a community that helped people live life with purpose, we could have a meaningful impact on the

world. From the moment we started, we had conviction that there was an entrepreneurial spirit that was underserved. We knew there were creators all around the world who were looking for a better workplace solution at a lower price."[36]

This idea proved a great fit for its times. At the time of the prospectus, We Company's largest business, WeWork, offered a "space as a service" membership model that grew to include shared work spaces in 111 cities. Other services, including insurance, education, technology, human resources and food, were offered through partnerships that made it easier to start a new business.

The prospectus suggested that the addressable market was 280 cities containing 255 million people and a total revenue opportunity of $3 trillion.[37] There was talk of "the WeWork effect".

The We Company's rapid growth consumed a large amount of capital at increasing valuations. By the time of the planned IPO, Reuters reported[38] that We Company had raised $12.8 billion in equity since its founding in 2010.

Yet the release of the IPO opened the business to the examination of a new group of investors and the general public. As is common in can-kicking episodes, this new group of observers were much less inclined to accept aspects of WeWork that appeared controversial: the founder's style; the prospect of related party transactions between the firm and the founder; a business model that was based on using short-term revenues to service long-term liabilities; and a business making increasing operating losses.

In late 2019, the *Financial Times* reported that We Company was valued at US$8 billion, less than the total equity contributed to the company to that date.[39]

Was this can-kicking? There were clearly underlying, long-lasting problems. Few outside the company appear to believe that the We

Company had built a business that was of lasting value. In the immediate aftermath of the failed IPO, the CEO and many executives have been replaced. There is a new chairman and Board members, and thousands of staff have been retrenched. Important aspects of the company's initial business model have been found wanting, including the company's willingness to take on long-term leases against short-run income streams. Evidence of the inner workings of We Company began to emerge, including the behaviours and relationships that drove We Company's choices. As this book was being finalised, WeWork recorded a US$2.1 billion loss in the first quarter of 2021, including the impact of the Covid pandemic as well as a US$500 million payment to founder Adam Neumann.[40] There was speculation of a new strategy and an acquisition by a special purpose acquisition company.[41]

It took exposure to outsiders to surface and address these problems. A Board of major investors, and a founder CEO with close confidants as senior executives, were unable to do so. Nor were the advisers on the IPO or, presumably, at other stages in the firm's evolution.

Alternatives to can-kicking

Can-kicking is a governance challenge because Board and senior management behaviour is central to it. Many of the characteristics of predictable surprises arise from known and manageable cognitive and organisational biases. Failing to manage these enables can-kicking. Worse, an impression that Boards are unwilling to hear about, and appropriately deal with, obvious or predictable performance issues can contribute to bad conduct and poor performance.

Picking up the "can" and dealing with it can create substantial value. For example, Amatil, once a cigarette company, could have kicked its dependence on smoking down the road. Instead the Board, led by executive chair Dean Wills, disposed of the cigarette business and reinvested in Coca-Cola franchises and other beverage businesses. In hindsight this move seems obvious. In practice, quitting a profitable business is a very tough call. Other examples of not kicking the can include BHP's move away from steel, and Wesfarmers' and Westfield's purchase, development and divestments across a range of businesses. Most recently, dependence on profits from fossil fuels may also create a potential can kicking arena for a number of firms.

Boards should be well positioned to help avoid predictable surprises. Bazerman and Watkins suggest avoidance requires:[42]

- scanning the environment for information regarding threats;
- integrating the information from multiple sources;
- responding in a timely manner;
- observing the results of response;
- incorporating lessons learned into "institutional memory"; and
- remaining alert to outside perspectives.

Our observation is that these are questions and actions that should be part of a Board's work, whether the issue appears on the conformance or the performance side of the ledger.

Chapter Three

Ethical and legal failures

The previous chapter dealt with governance failures that lead to poor performance. This chapter looks at two other kinds of failure – unethical conduct and clearly illegal activity, such as deliberate concealment of problems by management. Ethical and legal problems were very much the focus of the 2018-19 governance crisis as characterised by the Financial Services Royal Commission. The Commission and related inquiries suggest ethical breakdowns are more widespread than typically thought. Illegal behaviour is rarer, but its impact on shareholders, employees, customers and the communities that rely on an affected company can be substantial.

Unethical conduct

It has never been a good or sustainable business practice to behave unethically. Sadly, unethical business practices have been present for almost as long as business has been conducted.

Acting unethically towards customers and suppliers can be a route to increased rewards for both firms and executives, and these rewards can last for some time. The attraction to unscrupulous businesses and business people of selling products that cannot be used, continuing to charge materially more than the cost of an equivalent product the company also offers, failing to properly serve customers, or selling products and services that are clearly inappropriate for particular customers, is both clear and well-understood.

This attraction towards unethical behaviour, and its prevention, is central to the findings of the Financial Services Royal Commission. As we described in the Preface, Commissioner Hayne identified simple ethical failures at the core of many of the incidents he identified as being contrary to community expectations, and (at times) contrary to the law.

Volume 2 of Commissioner Hayne's final report included case studies of unethical behaviour from all major branches of the financial services sector. Some case studies have become notorious: the concept of "fees for no service" was widely reported during the Royal Commission.[43] This concept referred to superannuation fund trustees who allowed fees to be paid for advisers without monitoring whether those advisers had provided any services to fund members. Other case studies – for example those concerning issues where life insurance was sold to vulnerable consumers[44] or denied payments through conditions of coverage that did not match generally accepted medical standards[45] – were also associated with distressing personal circumstances.

Other examples identified by the Commission are in a sense less exploitative, but no less unethical. In superannuation there was the observed long-term practice (by both not-for-profit industry funds and for-profit retail funds) of default life-insurance as part of a superannuation product. This industry-wide practice of selling life insurance policies to young, single, part-time workers, while clearly profitable, systematically took advantage of customers who were legally required to acquire a product (superannuation) as a condition of their employment but had limited capacity to understand what they were purchasing.

An overarching impression from the Commission's final report is the prevalence of unethical behaviour in many parts of a diverse industry. The Commission identifies unethical conduct among superannuation trustees; financial advisers; superannuation investment managers; general and life insurers; bank branch staff; and superannuation service providers. Further case studies, published as part of the Commission Interim Report, identify unethical conduct by lenders and brokers who serve retail consumers, small and medium enterprises, agricultural producers and remote communities.

A second impression is that in many cases the actions and choices described in the reports were, in retrospect, clearly unethical. In the case of the life insurance examples described above, the Commission as well as a separate APRA investigation found that the delay in updating product conditions in line with industry norms and medical evidence was an explicit decision to disadvantage customers.[46] The simple realisation that these choices should be easy to make was encapsulated in the widely discussed question from the Royal Commission period: we can do this, but should we?

Commissioner Hayne's Final Report also identified four contributors to unethical behaviour.[47] These are:

- "The conduct in issue was driven not only by the relevant entity's pursuit of profit, but also by individuals' pursuit of gain… rewards have been paid whether the person rewarded should have done what they did.
- Entities and individuals acted in the ways they did because they could… There was a marked imbalance of power and knowledge between those providing the product or service and those acquiring it.
- Consumers often dealt with the financial services entity through an intermediary. The client might assume that the

person standing between the client and the entity that would provide a financial service or product acted for the client and in the client's interests. But in many cases, the intermediary is paid by, and may act in the interests of, the provider of the service or product.
- Too often, financial services entities that broke the law were not properly held to account."

These conditions are present beyond financial services; perhaps unsurprisingly, so is unethical conduct. Recent Australian examples include:

- Between 2013 and 2015, the ACCC fined AGL,[48] Energy Australia,[49] Australian Power and Gas,[50] Neighbourhood Energy[51] and Origin Energy[52] for inappropriate door-to-door marketing activities. (Origin, Energy Australia and AGL had stopped all door-to-door marketing in 2013.)
- Enrolment agents offering iPads or computer incentives to sign up students to educational institutions, funded by government, but who had no hope of graduating.

Deliberate concealment of bad outcomes

Major governance crises occur when management misleads the Board and is found out. However, identifying wilful deceit by a clever and charismatic CEO is almost impossible. Aggressive accounting to cover small performance issues is even harder to discover but can over time escalate to become insurmountable.

Put bluntly, Boards – like anybody – can be and are deceived. The flow of information coming to the Board is controlled by management. While most managers take their duty to properly inform the Board extremely seriously, there are times when management conceals performance issues it wants to keep away from the Board. This can happen when there is a performance or accounting problem that management hopes remedial action will fix. If the fix works, the Board will have had no awareness of the issue. But if the fix fails, management can end up in deeper water.

When this is believed to be happening, a common reaction of a Board member who feels they are not getting the full story is to resign, citing time pressures of other activities.

Two recent incidents – one famous, the other involving a famous firm – illustrate the challenge of deliberate deception.

Theranos

In a now celebrated tale, in 2003 Elizabeth Holmes, then 19 years old, dropped out of Stanford to start a new venture called Theranos. Her idea was to develop and commercialise technology that would perform a suite of accurate blood tests using only a few drops of blood, rather than a number of vials.

About US$700 million was raised by Theranos, which saw its value peak at about US$9 billion in 2013 and 2014.

However, the technology didn't work, and an increasingly desperate management began covering up failures and misleading potential partners, investors, customers and the Board of Directors.

In 2018, following an extensive investigation by John Carreyrou of the *Wall Street Journal*, the real story emerged, and the company was wound up, with no equity value. Criminal fraud charges were brought against Holmes.

Who were the directors and investors and what role did they play? The directors were a who's who of corporate America.

In May 2016, the Theranos Board comprised:

- Elizabeth Holmes, founder, CEO and Chair;

- Riley Bechtel, former Bechtel Group CEO;
- David Boies, a founder and the chairman of leading law firm Boies Schiller and Flexner;
- William Foege, a former director of the Centres for Disease Control and Prevention;
- Richard Kovacevich, former Wells Fargo CEO and chairman;
- James Mattis, later Secretary of Defence; and
- Fabrizio Bonanni, former executive vice-president of Amgen, a bio-pharmaceutical company.

Investors included Rupert Murdoch, the Cox family (owners of a private media and auto services conglomerate), and the Walton family (of Wal-Mart fame). Neither the Board nor investors insisted on an independent audit of the technology, and none was prepared. Whether it would have made a difference given the CEO's control of the Board and firm is questionable.

According to Carreyrou, Holmes saw the Board members as "ornaments", and when directors visited, staff were instructed not to make eye contact as this might lead to conversations that Holmes did not want to occur. When employees approached directors with concerns, they were fobbed off. When directors with concerns left the Board, they largely remained silent. Yet in terms of governance, all the relevant boxes could be ticked. The failure to dig deeply enough is not a crime. The absence of specific skills on the Board in this type of technology was countered by the eminence of the directors and their experience as investors.

Essentially, the high profile, senior Board was unable to penetrate the deception by the CEO.

Most of the standard prescriptions for "best practice" governance were in place. There was a clear majority of experienced independent directors, and an independent audit committee. The one governance weakness, though at the time common practice in the US, was Holmes' position as CEO and chair rather than the appointment of an independent non-executive chair. Yet a determined CEO could deceive numerous senior directors for 15 or so years. And when directors did become disenchanted, no loud whistles were blown.

General Electric

A more typical albeit relatively under-examined case is provided by the fall of General Electric, once America's premier company. GE's recent challenges have been well covered by the American business press.

Aggressive accounting at GE was a tradition that existed even in the glory days of CEO Jack Welch, who was famous for consistently just exceeding earnings expectations.

Later, when GE ran into serious difficulties, it stepped up the use of questionable accounting practices. For example, its power division offered customers discounts to extend service contracts on turbines and so increased the value of the service contracts – reporting this increased value as current year profit. But these were paper profits, leading to lower cash flows and lower profits in the future.

The assumed "get out of jail" card for GE was a resumption of historic growth in demand for these maintenance services for turbines. But the opposite occurred, with demand falling as production of renewable energy increased. In this example too, the Board did not effectively challenge the CEO, who had significant control over Board composition.

Why didn't effective governance identify this situation? As in the case of Theranos, GE had and has a stellar Board, but at the time it was very much under the control of the CEO and far too large. The *Wall Street Journal* reported that:[53]

> *"Board meetings at GE were an elaborate production. With 18 directors and another dozen regular attendees, the room was packed, and the agenda was, too. The plan being implemented in the first part of 2018 called for the Board's size to be cut to 12."*

As well as composition, the *Wall Street Journal* reported that atmospherics around the Board discouraged rigorous enquiry.

> *"One newcomer under Welch was so surprised by the lack of debate that the director asked a more senior colleague, 'what is the role of a GE Board member?' 'Applause,' the older director answered."*

Preventing failures of this type is a major concern for directors. One reason for this is their perceived and actual impact. Many prominent failures have this type of concealment at their core.

In addition, a lesson of history is that failures of this type are sufficiently regular to be of real concern. Finding examples of this type of governance failure is not difficult. As this book was being written Wirecard, a fast-growing European payments company, had cascaded from media scrutiny into criminal charges and widespread investigations about the firm and also advisers and regulators, and ultimately the insolvency of the company. This process began when the *Financial Times* reported it had found documents that "appear to indicate a concerted effort to fraudulently inflate sales and profits at Wirecard businesses in Dubai and Ireland". As subsequent events suggested, fraudulent practices at a recently acquired international unit within a fast growing, fast moving business may be the classic example of this type of governance challenge.

Closer to Australia, the collapse of Greensill Capital and the findings from a range of enquiries into Crown Casinos provide examples of directors, investors, lenders and others missing or failing to gather information to assess material business risks, and matters of legal and ethical conduct.

There is also no obvious way to avoid deliberate concealment. It is not sufficient to be part of a Board with prominent, apparently well-qualified colleagues. Directors on the Theranos Board could take no comfort from the prominence and apparent qualifications of their colleagues. There is also the challenge of how best to interrogate an important but invisible (to the Board) business problem.

Prevention is also difficult. Motives for this type of misconduct are varied and powerful. One of management's motives in concealing bad outcomes is to inflate the results on which their remuneration is based. Another motive is to buy time for a high-risk strategy that the Board would likely not have approved.

A final and related issue can be the unwillingness of directors to push back and question the CEO. There is a lot of truth in the saying "the longer you wait to ask, the dumber your question sounds". Because of the large gap in knowledge between management and part-time directors, directors can feel uncomfortable asking "dumb questions". Directors are also often concerned not to develop a reputation of being "difficult", as this can limit future invitations to join other Boards.

As a result, Boards can fail to appropriately question management on even important issues – particularly those likely to place the Board in direct conflict with senior management. This is especially likely when the Board is asked to spend increasing amounts of time on large numbers of routine issues unrelated to performance.

Glib invitations for Board members just to "ask better questions" ignore these pressures which are sufficiently powerful to impact even highly qualified Boards.

One approach that Boards have found helpful is to designate one or two directors to be "black hats" on an issue. The black hat's job is to raise questions that a director may be uncomfortable raising without the cover of explicit expectations.

Finally, how do these overly aggressive accounting treatments or outright frauds slip past the Board Audit Committee and its external auditor? These ethical and legal failures still occur despite these two major specialist efforts aimed at their detection and prevention.

Audit committees that rely on inquiry of management are of course bound by the quality of information they receive. At face value there should be quantitative evidence of problems. But of course, in the most blatant cases management either conceals information or tells lies, for example about balance sheet values. There is also misinformation on a small scale that can escalate. In these cases, the problem can begin with "aggressive accounting", for example in the valuation of assets, especially financial assets that are marked to market. Aggressive revenue recognition is another concern. If management is lucky and performance improves, the aggressive approach will no longer be needed and can be quietly reversed. But if the business problem that triggered the aggressive accounting gets worse, management either needs even more aggressive accounting, or comes clean with severe career consequences.

The value of external audit in preventing this type of action is increasingly uncertain, and itself the subject of pressure to improve performance.

Combined, these circumstances have a clear implication: current governance approaches find outright deception difficult to systematically address.

* * *

The type of outright unethical behaviour that has brought about Australia's latest governance crisis was and is unacceptable. Boards need to embrace the challenge of reducing bad conduct and making amends when it occurs.

But the governance challenge before directors is broader and more persistent than unethical conduct. Consequently, it is more threatening to the sustainability of the listed sector than is typically acknowledged.

Improving governance also means addressing the other types of governance failures that are equally damaging to listed firms: deliberate concealment of bad outcomes; kicking-the-can on major performance or strategy problems rather than facing up to them; and willingness to accept marginal performance at the expense of both customers and shareholders.

The remainder of this book explains why we believe the current approaches to governance are inadequate to meet these challenges, and prescribes remedies to overcome them.

PART II

More-of-the-same won't work

Our analyses and interviews have led us to conclude that the current approach to improving governance, which we characterise as more-of-the-same, needs a fundamental rethink, not fine tuning.

In Part II, we argue that the four major governance failures persist because most governance reform ideas amount to more-of-the-same. By this we mean that the direction of these reforms is to build from supposed best practice in a way that adds more constraints to the way in which Boards are constructed and operate.

Describing how this is happening in corporate governance is the purpose of Part II. We ask: "is the current direction of travel in public governance the right one?" We explore the question in Chapter Four, reviewing how more-of-the-same has arisen in the governance debate, and argue its overriding impact has emphasised process over substance. In Chapter Five we examine four very common, specific implementations of more-of-the-same, and argue they do not effectively address the four types of governance failures we have described.

Chapter Four

The genesis of more-of-the-same

The main tenets of what is believed to be good governance for publicly listed firms are laid down in the listing rules of key stock exchanges.

In Australia, these best practice governance principles are developed by the ASX Corporate Governance Council. The principles have been updated every three or four years since their introduction in 2003. The way the principles take effect is through the ASX requirement that listed entities either comply with the principles or, if not, explain why not.[54] The intention of this approach was clear when established. The principles were by definition generic and therefore it was the responsibility of each listed entity to find an appropriate application of the principles to the specifics of their context. It should also be remembered that these principles are to guide a highly diverse range of companies: in size – enormous versus tiny; in maturity – early-stage versus mature; and in nature – covering every industry imaginable. A summary of the ASX governance principles is set out in Appendix 2.

There are three important observations/trends in relation to these principles:

1. They emphasise conformance rather than performance. Phrases such as "achieving excellence", "effectively innovating" or "displaying resilience" are absent.
2. With each revision these conformance-orientated principles and their accompanying notes become increasingly detailed. The development and use of a skills matrix, discussed later, is a case in point.
3. Most worryingly, what were initially set out to be guidelines are increasingly being treated as implicit rules: any divergence, even when explained, is unlikely to be tolerated by large shareholders and proxy advisers.

The unintended yet very real consequence of these accumulating factors is a situation where public company governance has gone long on conformance-related issues, rigidly defined. As a result, it becomes practical wisdom amongst directors that if (when) a governance problem emerges, those who supported a divergence from the guidance are at risk of being blamed for supporting less than best-practice good governance. This, increasingly, is interpreted as non-compliance. The fact that the reasons for these choices were clearly explained and even agreed to via a vote of shareholders may offer little protection. Rather, mechanistically adhering to the guidelines becomes the safer option for a Board in a conformance orientated environment.

The overall direction of travel in public company governance is in effect asking Boards to improve governance by doing more-of-the-same: to focus largely on conformance matters, in increasingly prescriptive detail, and with less tolerance of diversity in their application. This is accompanied by an unstated but in practice clear change to emphasise the compliance with guidelines over the flexibility to adapt to circumstances.

The fact that revisions to the principles tend to propose changes at the margin is not disputed. In an interview with the Australian Institute of Company Directors, ASX Corporate Governance Council Chair Elizabeth Johnstone described changes in the fourth edition as "evolutionary, not revolutionary".[55] Or, to quote from former Business Council of Australia chairman Graham Bradley's 2019 Bathurst Lecture, "our corporate law and governance is fundamentally sound… it is a model to be nurtured and preserved not subverted".[56]

Our concern is with the direction of travel, not the pace.

The emphasis on compliance with guidelines over flexibility to adapt to circumstances is not only an Australian phenomenon. As US business academics Larcker and Tayan describe, although "there are no universally agreed-upon standards for good governance … this has not stopped blue ribbon panels from recommending uniform standards to market participants".[57] In the UK, for example, the Cadbury report was followed by another six reports on corporate governance practices over the next 20 years.[58] Each of these inquiries focussed their recommendations on modest enhancements to current governance norms, without tying their recommendations to the corporate governance failures we have identified.

More recently, in a submission to the UK Financial Reporting Council's inquiry into the UK Corporate Governance Code,[59] BlackRock, a leading fund manager, notes that it:

> ***"[S]hares the FRC's view that, over time, focus has shifted away from understanding the principles which underpin good corporate governance and demonstrating intent to adhere to these principles."***

They also note that although "flexibility should be at the heart of corporate governance" this "guiding principle has become somewhat diluted by the number of prescriptive parameters added by multiple revisions to the UK Corporate Governance Code".

Our own interviews with directors strongly reinforced this view. There was a collective sense that their time was being increasingly caught up in ensuring process was met and documented, rather than thinking deeply about confronting the more difficult issues facing the company either from a performance or conformance perspective.

A corollary of this view is that being a director is less satisfying than was the case 20 or so years ago. What made the role fun was dealing with real opportunities and problems in an environment of effective collaboration.

The evidence for more-of-the-same

If this more-of-the-same approach coupled with increased compliance was effective, we would expect to see a reduction in governance failures. We would also expect an improvement in the performance of firms complying with the principles compared with those that did not comply. However, this does not seem to be the lived reality. The recent reviews of the Royal Commission, ASIC and APRA, and their findings of numerous governance failures in leading firms, suggest the principles as written, reported upon, and acted upon are not helpful.

While this is an uncomfortable implication for supporters of the current best practice approach, it should not be surprising. The NYSE Corporate Governance Guide,[60] drawing on research by Stanford University, includes the table set out below. It conveys a clear message that best practice is a point of view, not a research-supported, evidence-based set of rules.

Board attribute	Explanation	Findings from research
Independent chairman	The chairman of the Board meets NYSE standards for independence	No evidence that this matters
Lead independent director	The Board has designated an independent director as the lead person to represent the independent directors in conversation with management, shareholders and other stakeholders	Modest evidence that this improves performance
Number of outside directors	Number of directors who come from outside the company (non-executive)	Mixed evidence that this can improve performance and reduce agency costs. Depends primarily on how difficult it is for outsiders to acquire expert knowledge of the company and its operations
Number of independent directors	Number of directors who meet NYSE standards for independence	No evidence that this matters beyond a simple majority
Independence of committees	Board committees are entirely made up of directors who meet NYSE standards for independence	Positive impact on earnings quality for audit committee only. No evidence for other committees

This missing connection between best practice and evidence appears completely lost in the current debate about corporate governance. Of course, the absence of evidence does not negate the validity of a sound principle where the research has not been conducted. However, where research has been done and there is little evidence of correlation, yet alone causation, then the way in which such principles are being positioned as prescriptive rules must be questioned.

The origin of "best practice" is as obscure as its application is widespread. Researching its application in education, Larry Cuban of the Stanford Graduate School of Education writes:

> *"Where does the phrase 'best practice' originate? I checked around the blogosphere and its origin seems to be in the business sector with management consultants and corporate gurus. It has become a buzzword across government, education and medical organisations."*

Professor Cuban notes:

> *"In becoming popular, the phrase has drifted away linguistically from its original meaning of effective practices in accomplishing goals to mean faddish or trendy activities."*

Finally, he draws on research in the medical field to suggest that a common failing of best practice is that the experts who recommended them:

> *"[D]id not distinguish between medical practices that can be standardised and not significantly altered by the condition of the individual patient, and those that must be adapted to a particular person."*

In short, best practices can inadvertently lead to a focus on universal conformance without an appropriate evidence base.

Emphasis on process versus outcomes

The overriding impact of the more-of-the-same concept has been an emphasis on process versus outcomes across almost every area of Board construction and operation.

This was the most common complaint from our discussions with chairs and directors. Their experience was of an enormous tide of advice that compliance with process is, if not a sign of governance excellence, then a sign of appropriate governance practice. At times, complying with processes was also seen as delivering protection against potential legal liabilities.

A focus on process is reflected in much of the language in the corporate governance standards. Principle 1 of the ASX guide states that a listed entity should: "lay solid foundations for management and oversight" and "clearly delineate the respective roles of its Board and management ...".

Role clarity is clearly a good thing. However, having a statement along the lines of principle doesn't mean that the statement reflects what really happens, and how what really happens helps or hinders performance. None of the "principles" require a commitment to excellence in terms of results and management quality. Similar comments could be made about other principles. For example, many can be satisfied by "box ticking", such as reporting that requisite committees with requisite independence are in place, and meet with requisite regularity.

The audit committee, one of the more critical pieces of governance, provides another example. Recommendation 4.1 of the ASX Corporate Governance Guidelines states that the Board of a listed entity should:

a. Have an audit committee which:
   1. has at least three members, all of whom are non-executive directors and a majority of whom are independent directors;
   2. is chaired by an independent director, who is not the chair of the board;

and disclose:

3. the charter of the committee;
4. the relevant qualifications and experience of the members of the committee; and
5. in relation to each reporting period, the number of times the committee met throughout the period and the individual attendances of the members at those meetings; or

b. if it does not have an audit committee, disclose that fact and the processes it employs that independently verify and safeguard the integrity of its corporate reporting, including the processes for the appointment and removal of the external auditor and the rotation of the audit engagement partner.

However, the recommendation is silent on the role of the committee, and the elements and drivers of good performance. Research on the effectiveness of audit committees suggests this is an important missing element. In a study of how audit can support corporate governance, Jeffrey Cohen and Arnold Wright, academics at Boston College, and Ganesh Krishnamoorthy from Northwestern University, find:

> *"[D]espite the attention placed on the audit committee in the academic literature, in the business community and by regulators in different countries (e.g. Canada, United States, Australia) several respondents indicated that their experiences with their clients suggest that audit committees are typically ineffective and lack sufficient power to be a strong governance mechanism."*

In the case of this research, the respondents were auditors reflecting on client experiences. The authors of the research report that "auditors view management as the primary driver of corporate governance", not the Board.

In an environment where directors feel under significant personal as well as collective pressure, focussing on process has considerable practical appeal. While no Board or director can have complete control over business outcomes, it is possible to have complete control over whether a process is completed as defined – particularly when process definition is itself within the control of the Board. Without a predisposition towards governance principles that prefer outcomes, who can blame directors for preferring this lower risk option, at least in the short term.

This is one element of more-of-the-same where the tide of opinion has begun to turn. In its investigation into how Australian firms manage non-financial risks, ASIC acknowledged that it "has been concerned that corporate reporting on governance has suffered from a form over substance approach, with an emphasis on frameworks and processes rather than actual practices". Examples provided by ASIC included:

- Although many directors identified non-financial risks as a concern "there was no strong corresponding trend of directors actually seeking out adequate data or reporting that informed them of their overall exposure," or evidence that directors actively engaged with information they received.
- Some companies had Board approved risk appetite statements in place, but management operated outside these for years at a time with the tacit acceptance of the Board.
- Directors agreeing and then ignoring descriptions of their own responsibility. ASIC "saw Boards approving charters governing the operation of [Board Risk Committees]; however the Boards did not hold themselves accountable to operating in accordance with those charters".

These examples appear to be process over substance by choice, not by accident.

Process over outcomes and governance failures

More to the point, the emphasis on process is unlikely to remedy the governance failures discussed in Chapters Two and Three. Acceptance of marginal performance and can-kicking are not mentioned in the governance guidelines. Values and ethics are included in the governance principles (Principle 3) but the prevalence of unethical conduct in the numerous regulatory reviews suggests the principles remain difficult to turn into practical countermeasures. Finally, more process will not address the structural imbalances in time, information flow and in-depth knowledge that lie at the heart of deliberate concealment of bad news.

Chapter Five

More-of-the-same in practice

More-of-the-same has had, and without change will have, specific impacts on governance practices. Four specific areas that we describe as more-of-the-same are:

1. a heightened focus on mechanistically defined director "independence";
2. director selection increasingly orientated towards technical competencies as described in a skills matrix;
3. increased disclosure to the Board and by the Board; and
4. loading the Board with additional conformance tasks in areas felt to be getting insufficient attention.

To illustrate the practical impacts of more-of-the-same, we now examine each of these elements in turn.

Heightened focus on mechanistically defined independence

An independent director is typically defined as being one "free from conflicts of interests that might compromise their ability to solely act in the interest of the firm".

According to the ASX Corporate Governance Principles "to describe a director as 'independent' carries with it a particular connotation that the director is not aligned with the interests of management or a substantial holder and will bring an independent judgement to bear on issues before the Board. It is an appellation that gives great comfort to security holders and not one that should be applied lightly."

Corporate governance guidelines for listed firms define with some precision, and broadly in the same terms, eligibility tests for independent directors (see Box 5.1 for the ASX version). These tests require independent directors to limit the extent to which their income is or has been derived from the firm on which they serve. At times a specific size limit on this income is set; on other occasions judgements about materiality are left open to the firm. A financial relationship with or being a proxy of a substantial shareholder, being a substantial shareholder (usually with more than 5-10 per cent of the stock), and/or former employment with the company (usually within three years), are all examples of specific circumstances that are formally considered incompatible with independence. So too is length of service as a director, the assumption being that those with long service are captured by management or by their own past judgements or decisions, and so will not be able to view new issues dispassionately.

This ignores the contribution based on longer term involvement with the company that a long serving director may bring. In a board of eight to 10 members, having two directors with long tenure can add a longer-term perspective to balance prevalent short-termism.

Current independence tests may not work

The challenge posed by these definitions is whether these standards produce directors who will in practice be i) more motivated to exercise independent judgement in the interests of all shareholders and

ii) have the requisite knowledge, experience and temperament to raise and discuss key issues with management and each other in a collegial and constructive way.

Most studies fail to find a significant relationship between meeting the current tests of director independence and improved corporate outcomes, and suggest other tests would be more appropriate. Two widely cited , deliberately designed studies are:

- Research by Purdue University academics Byoung-Hyoun Hwang and Seoyoung Kim in 2009 that demonstrated the relevance of a director's social circle (a measure at the time absent in definitions of independence) as an important factor in independence considerations. They found that between 1996 and 2005 around 25 per cent of Fortune 100 directors met NYSE independence standards but not important indicators of social independence from the CEO. This in turn correlated with higher executive compensation, lower CEO turnover after poor performance, and a higher likelihood that the CEO manipulates earnings to increase his or her bonus.
- Similarly, US Business School academics Jeffrey Coles, Naveen Daniel and Lalitha Naveen found that the greater the percentage of the Board appointed during the current CEO's tenure, the worse a Board performs its monitoring function; meaning that the timing of when a director was appointed relative to the CEO was a greater explanatory factor on outcomes than the underlying measure of independence itself. A possible reason is that a director appointed while the CEO holds office may feel beholden to the CEO, who must have been supportive of the appointment.

Consistent with these findings about social independence, Boston College academics William Stevenson and Robert Radin found that directors who have social ties and meet outside of the Boardroom are also more influential over the Board.

The principle that the fiduciary duty of a director is to act at all times in the interests of the firm is clear; all directors are required to act independently of their personal interests. The question imposed by the research is: how do increasingly prescriptive definitions of independence assist in meeting this governance challenge?

Independent directors, by meeting defined independence standards, are assumed to be able to put the interests of the corporation ahead of their own. From this perspective, they should make for good monitors of the firm. Independent directors are considered most useful for evaluating the performance of the firm's executive team and for overseeing the firm's disclosures. For example, one study from Singapore Management University shows that when Boards comprise more independent directors, material weaknesses in internal controls are more quickly remediated.

However, being free from conflicts is not sufficient for quality monitoring. An effective monitoring function also requires knowledge: in particular knowledge about the firm's industry, its operations and strategies, as well as about practices such as executive pay setting and auditing. Independence without knowledge therefore comes with some trade-offs.

Directors are also not just responsible for monitoring the firm; they are also expected to provide advice to senior management. Providing advice, like monitoring, also requires knowledge. Research, however, cautions that monitoring and providing advice may not be activities that easily coexist. Boards that monitor intensively (for example, terminate CEOs when firm performance is poor, prevent excessive CEO compensation, etc) tend to have a majority of independent directors. However, these same firms appear to be under-served on the advice side. Research by US academics Oulbunmi Faleye, Rani Hoitash and

Udi Hoitash finds a strong focus on monitoring is associated with underperformance when acquiring other firms and in innovation. Importantly, this research concludes "that the negative advising effects outweigh the benefits of improved monitoring, especially when acquisitions or corporate innovation are significant value drivers or the firm's operations are complex".

Concordia University Accountancy Fellow Professor Claudine Mangen describes a summary of what is known about director independence – one that hardly supports current approaches to independence:

1. Independence alone is not enough. In order for independent directors to be effective monitors, they need to be knowledgeable about the company, its environment, and its transactions. Independence therefore becomes less impactful where the cost of relevant knowledge is high. And they need the experience and personal attributes to sense when to push hard and when to back off while keeping deliberations polite and constructive. These qualities only become apparent after appointment, when options to deal with a non-performing director are limited.
2. Overweighting director independence can be counter-productive: independent directors who are good monitors tend to give less good advice. As such, it is important to know what matters more for a particular firm: a Board that monitors management or a Board that advises management.
3. What matters in terms of director independence to a particular firm depends on its context. This includes societal circumstances (e.g., is there a sufficient a pool of directors from which to recruit?), its economic environment (e.g., is it growing fast, does it have to innovate?), and its governance situation (e.g. does it have an influential CEO, or an informative stock price?).

Independence issues outside the current approach

Even if the link between current tests and independent behaviour was strong, by focussing only on mechanistic rules Boards cannot address important current independence issues.

One is the rise of the career director. This is a very live issue amongst the directors we interviewed, and in many cases the subject of substantial concern. These directors are characterised as people who leave their first careers early, typically from professional services such as law, accounting or finance, to become company directors as a career, rather than a semi-retirement give-back. With three significant Board appointments, career directors can earn north of $700,000 per annum, competitive with their alternative high-pressure professional jobs. However, the sustainability of this emerging career path and its very relevant income stream can be put at risk if the director becomes seen as "difficult" by colleagues, with future invitations to join new Boards drying up. Taking on the chair, CEO or a senior executive role can become career limiting for these directors. Career directors could be an important source of new talent in the director pool, but only if they can safely exert their independence.

A second issue is whether current director remuneration, typically flat fees unrelated to performance, helps or hinders effective independence. Flat fees related to firm performance avoid the problem of directors both setting and benefitting from quite complex definitions of performance. However, this flat fee form of remuneration is only weakly aligned with shareholder interests.

Some of the highest order goals of a Board – including that management appropriately protects and adds long-term value to shareholder funds – appear consistent with and supported by increased levels of share ownership by directors, more so than director fees unrelated to performance.

Fees unrelated to performance, according to our interviewees, do make more sense if they are paid out as, say, 50 per cent cash and 50 per cent shares that must be held for five or so years. At current levels of Board fees in major companies, directors would hold about $1 million of shares after five years. Alignment with the interests of all shareholders should then be quite strong.

When choice is available, many firms prefer directors to be compensated through a combination of fees, equity or equity options, and any increase in the value of the shares directors own. A number of CEOs we spoke to clearly prefer their directors to have a substantial shareholding. In other markets this is common: in 2020 stock grants were 57 per cent of director compensation across the S&P 500.

Mechanistically-defined independence and governance failures

Exchanges' guidelines outline the interests that raise issues about a director's independence, and are therefore long on negative tests that rely on minimum standards and disclosure.

What is missing from these guidelines, however, is a statement of the attributes that describe and underpin effective and genuine independence. The main point in the principles is that the director has had no commercial or employment relationship with the firm for three years prior to appointment. Without any balancing statements in favour of independence, this trade-off seems to settle on the wrong side of ticking a box versus enabling judgement about character and independence of mind. This is particularly problematic when directors with relevant knowledge of the company and its business are scarce.

Without these statements, best practice guidelines can't help Boards create the conversations and thought processes that will be needed to improve performance or conformance. Of course, chairs and directors can define these requirements for themselves – hoping of course that a growing collection of independence requirements doesn't rule out the best minds they could otherwise recruit.

Clearly, if a director needs their role for their financial or other wellbeing, they are less likely to act independently. Once this test has been passed, governance would be improved if Boards had more freedom to choose the best available talent.

Box 5.1 ASX Corporate Governance Council's Principles and Recommendations 4th Edition February 2019

Factors relevant to assessing the independence of a director

Examples of interests, positions and relationships that might raise issues about the independence of a director of an entity include if the director:

- is, or has been, employed in an executive capacity by the entity or any of its child entities, and there has not been a period of at least three years between ceasing such employment and serving on the board;
- receives performance-based remuneration (including options or performance rights) from, or participates in an employee incentive scheme of, the entity;
- is, or has been within the last three years, in a material business relationship (e.g. as a supplier, professional adviser, consultant or customer) with the entity or any of its child entities, or is an officer of, or otherwise associated with, someone with such a relationship;
- is, or represents, or has been within the past three years an officer or employee of, or professional adviser to, a substantial holder;
- has close personal ties with any person who falls within any of the categories described above; or
- has been a director of the entity for such a period that their independence from management and substantial holders may have been compromised.

In each case, the materiality of the interest, position or relationship needs to be assessed by the Board to determine whether it might interfere, or might reasonably be seen to interfere, with the director's capacity to bring an independent judgement to bear on issues before the Board and to act in the best interests of the entity as a whole rather than in the interests of an individual security holder or other party.

Skills matrix versus independent judgement

Introduced as a means of assisting both Boards (by codifying/assessing the capability needs and capacity of directors) and shareholders (by disclosing to inform and give confidence), the skills matrix is a relatively new and rapidly developing example of more-of-the-same.

We want to take some time to spell out the evolution of the skills matrix because it is a specific example of how the more-of-the-same process occurs, and like independence, it goes to the heart of how directors should be chosen.

In neither the first (2003) nor second (2007) editions of the ASX guidelines was there mention of a skills matrix. Rather, the clear guidance was that "the Board should comprise directors possessing an appropriate range of skills and expertise".

However, in 2010 the third edition saw the introduction of a "skills matrix" as a formal recommendation (Recommendation 2.2) requiring both its existence and disclosure. The recommendation is that:

> *"A listed entity should have and disclose a Board skills matrix setting out the mix of skills and diversity that the Board currently has or is looking to achieve in its membership."*

The accompanying guidance suggested the matrix could be in the form of a description of current or desired skills (or both) and could exclude certain skill requirements that may be commercially sensitive. The reason given for the requirement ("it is a useful tool") and its disclosure ("useful information for investors and increases the accountability of the Board on such matters") are hard to argue with, but equally not clearly linked to desired standards or outcomes.

Having established this requirement in the Third Edition, the Fourth Edition (2019) extended what was required. This edition recommended that a Board "should regularly review its skills matrix" and "whichever format it follows, it would be helpful to investors for the entity to explain what it means when it refers to a particular skill in its Board skills matrix and the criteria a director must meet to be considered to have that skill". The guidelines also suggest that the form of a matrix is increasingly set, telling Boards that "guidance on what should be included in a Board skills matrix can be found in the Governance Institute of Australia's Good Governance Guide 'Creating and disclosing a Board skills matrix'."

Like the ASX Corporate Governance Guidelines, the Good Governance Guide provides more definition about the matrix, but leaves open many questions about the skills matrix. The Guide:

- Suggests "[i]t is good governance for a company to create a skills matrix in relation to its Board of Directors", although there is no evidence for this.
- Reinforces that "the inclusion of a skills matrix is required in the annual report for listed companies".
- Provides a non-exhaustive list of 19 possible desirable skills, 12 of which are related to specific subject matter expertise (e.g., accounting, marketing).

Unresolved questions, albeit with implicit recommendations, are:

- How to assess skills, including that a Board should "consider whether it wishes to give a weighting to the skills, experience, knowledge and capabilities of directors, through the use of a ratings system, such as 'High', 'Medium' and 'Low' and/or whether this has been gained in a management or non-executive context".
- How to disclose specific skills of individual directors, suggesting

that "[i]f the company discloses the specific skills it has identified as desirable, it needs to consider if it will specify how many directors hold those skills and whether to identify those directors".

- How to avoid revealing commercially sensitive information, suggesting "there can be a tension between the transparency needed to provide insight to Board thinking and the need to ensure that any disclosure of gaps in Board skills is not seen as detrimental to the company".
- Whether the matrix would increase liability of directors if a governance or business problem occurred in an area of their nominated skills.

What are Boards and directors to make of this? Both the ASX's and the Governance Institute of Australia's guidelines acknowledge the need for skills matrixes to be developed and applied in the context of a firm's circumstances. Equally, it is now clear that governance best practice is to have and disclose a skills matrix, and that this is likely to be focussed on the type of easily evidenced skills that can be proven through reference to past roles or qualifications.

We can understand why the skills matrix is attractive to professionals who help create and execute director selection processes, but it is less clear to us that it should be supported by those who want improved governance, including directors who want to be on high-performing Boards.

There is no evidence that the matrix's original and still most important governance objective, that "the Board should comprise directors possessing an appropriate range of knowledge and expertise" improves governance.

Given this direction of travel, the logical endpoint will be a very formalised matching of required Board skills with individual directors, possibly alongside a metric of their competency. Over time, there may be a requirement for the independent assessment of both skill needs and director competency of a Board; doing so today would be considered entirely consistent with current guidelines, and indeed could be seen as a helpful protection against biased self-assessments.

This approach is based on two underlying beliefs about what makes a high performing Board. Each of these is problematic.

The first is a belief that Board quality can be improved by technical methods of defining and assessing director eligibility and quality. Directors with concrete qualifications or specific, technical expertise more easily fit within this framework; those with more generic skills or general business experience even at the highest level less so. For example, in the skills named in the Governance Institute of Australia's guidance, there is no mention of sound judgement, independence of thought, strong ethics or interpersonal skills – arguably four of the most important skills of any public company director. Excluded also is the idea that industry experience and knowledge has a role to play in governance. This goes against common sense, and also a finding by the NY Stock Exchange (see Table 4.1) that the ability to secure knowledge of this type was a driver of the value of directors from inside the firm.

The second is that Boards must include directors that embody sufficient breadth of technical skills to address a Board agenda because Board agendas are (or should be) dominated by questions that are largely technical in nature. The evidence that this will address the most important governance challenges is not only missing, it also does not match well to the lived experience of many experienced directors we spoke with.

The experiences and knowledge that best equip directors for the type of thinking, conversations and debates required to govern large publicly listed enterprises – the nose to identify and address problems, the ability to assess people, the capacity to know how to constructively escalate an issue (be it performance or conformance related) – do not lend themselves to technically orientated skills matrices. Boards can easily create and meet a reasonably argued skills matrix. But creating this matrix does not prioritise the avoidance of any, or all, of the governance failures we have identified.

Practically, this increasingly detailed process, its disclosure and review appears to be another tick-the-box conformance task that adds little meaningful value but will inevitably increase risks to directors if they choose not to or are seen not to comply. The increased detailing of how to now meet and manage against this good governance requirement is yet another example of more-of-the-same thinking with a conformance focus.

Increased disclosure to the Board and by the Board

A fourth reform from the stable of more-of-the-same is increased disclosure by management to the Board, and by the Board and management to shareholders, which in effect means the public, including media, competitors, and others. The logic behind calls for more and more insightful disclosures is a version of "sunlight is the best disinfectant".

Where it is clear through insightful disclosures that the Board is tolerating marginal performance, can-kicking or concealing problems, action to remedy the situation is more likely.

The weakness of the reliance on disclosure to get the Board to address performance problems is that the volume of disclosures seems to trump the insightfulness of disclosures. In many cases, less can be more, but what happens instead is that "more is less".

Volume trumps insight

In interview after interview, directors we spoke with reported a substantial increase in the amount of written material put to Boards: 1000-page Board packs are not unheard of, particularly when sensitive areas such as finance, risk and remuneration are covered in a single meeting. Quantitative data on Board materials is difficult to obtain, but the recent ASIC report into non-financial risks reflects the views of the directors we spoke to, and our own experiences: many Board meetings now discuss hundreds of pages of written materials, often in meetings lasting two to three days.

Partly driven by legal obligations, directors are expected to be across this material at a significant level of detail, especially where the information concerns risk and compliance. As a director, one does not need much imagination to be wary of finding oneself in some future royal commission or class action being cross-examined by an SC asking, "and exactly what did you think about the implications of the statement found in paragraph four on page 445 of the August Board papers…?" In contrast, documents on important commercial and strategic matters can be brief, often of low quality, and, particularly after prior stringent legal review (now a requirement by some companies), apt to leave much unsaid. For directors, the sheer rise in volume can obviously be thought to be unsustainable simply from a pure bandwidth perspective.

Sole source information on performance

Even as the volume of disclosure grows, the source of most, if not all, of the disclosure provided to the Board remains management.

Discussion on the creation of alternative sources of information on performance is rare – yet it seems very clear that finding a way for the Board to observe directly the behaviour of their firm's products and staff as they serve customers would – almost by definition – considerably improve disclosure. Net Promotor Scores collected through standardised surveys and reported on by management have become a common approach for providing Board insights into customer satisfaction. Like all tools, they have their place, but their increasing ubiquity in Board reports can at times seem to be more a nod at ticking the box on meeting some disclosure need, rather than an attempt to provide material insights into some of the most important customer issues.

Other approaches are possible. Netflix takes a radically different approach to information sharing with the goal of significantly and efficiently increasing transparency among the CEO, executive team and Board of Directors. The Netflix approach incorporates two distinctive practices: (1) Board members periodically attend (in an observing capacity only) monthly and quarterly senior management meetings; and (2) Board communications are structured as approximately 30-page online memos in narrative form that not only include links to supporting analysis but also allow open access to all data and information on the company's internal shared systems, including the ability to ask clarifying questions of the subject authors.

Founder and CEO Reed Hastings believes these two practices improve the ability of the Board to provide what he calls an "extreme duty of care" to the corporation. The Board isn't going to have the confidence to make hard decisions unless they really understand the market and company.

Our inquiries suggest the current disclosure environment is travelling away from what experienced directors believe would best assist sound governance: insightful, open, reliable disclosures focussed on key issues – good as well as bad.

Executive remuneration – a case study about disclosure

Perhaps nowhere has the principle that more disclosure will lead to better outcomes been more publicly and aggressively applied than in executive remuneration.

The public perception of governance of large corporates is tightly linked to perceptions of the level and structure of executive remuneration.

This issue came sharply into focus during the Financial Services Royal Commission. In Volume 1 of the Commission's Final Report, Commissioner Kenneth Hayne expends considerable effort to unpick and assess the remuneration of senior executives at a number of financial institutions. During the Commission's hearings this issue attracted considerable attention, not least through reporting of the examination of the CBA Chair by counsel assisting the Commission. While the Commissioner described this evidence as an "instructive" example, the Commission's final report goes much further than a single incident. It describes well the general challenges and – in some cases – unsatisfactory elements of current remuneration approaches. This treatment readily extends beyond financial services.

Remuneration of executives has always been central to governance. Alignment of incentives is a crucial component of even the best monitoring and decision-making processes.

Remuneration has been impacted negatively by the current disclosure requirements. Published remuneration reports set out pay structure and amounts in considerable detail.

With executive pay made public, community and media "outrage" makes for good press, especially when standards of conduct and remuneration outcomes diverge. However, public reporting adds to pay inflation, as no Board or CEO wants executives to be paid less than similarly performing competitors. A counterproductive corollary is that a Board's discretion to give a sharp message via remuneration is limited, since a very public cut in pay raises the issue of whether the affected CEO or executive is "on the way out". As this is a bad way to convey such a message – if that was what is intended – it is no surprise that Boards don't spend much time on remuneration, particularly when the recommendation is similar to past decisions.

Additional disclosure has also failed to address – and arguably begun to embed as standard arrangements – inappropriate structural characteristics of remuneration schemes.

Public firm remuneration practices appear to be failing basic research supported tests of best practice. The sharing of firm out-performance is increasingly biased to executives over shareholders. Overall, executive remuneration is growing faster than excess returns to shareholders and pay increases to middle management and front-line workers. A number of directors expressed discomfort with how remuneration is handled, but a better approach is not obvious.

Loading the Board with additional tasks

The final area of more-of-the-same is loading the Board with additional tasks. Additional effort is a time-honoured remedy for governance performance below standard.

When a Board is seen to have not done what is expected, or not addressed a governance failure, the most common recommendation is to prescribe "more time" be spent on the area of concern, by the Board and/or the relevant committee.

There are four problems with asking the Board to take on new or expanded roles.

First, where will the time come from? *Strictly Boardroom* noted, 25-plus years ago, that expanded compliance duties were driving down the time spent on key drivers of performance such as company strategy. If anything, our interviews led us to believe that the situation is now even worse. More recent surveys of directors find lack of time to review and discuss strategy is a key governance weakness. The current call for even more expanded Board roles would create further problems.

Second, how will the Board's expanded role affect the relationship between Board and management? Having multiple non-executive directors for example as committee chairs, all interacting with the CEO and/or designated senior executives, further blurs the boundaries between the Board and management, and can erode the position of the CEO.

Third, what is the Board's most constructive approach in taking on broader roles? Should it consider and approve, or should it participate in formulation? Should it seek independent advice and if so, when and how?

Fourth, how do those who recommend simply spending additional time on a broader range of key issues expect performance to improve – without other major reforms designed to make Boards more effective?

To illustrate the challenges posed by simply choosing to do more, we examine specific examples of emerging issues with important governance implications.

Meaningfully addressing purpose in a more-of-the-same world

Corporate purpose is a live matter for Boards, one that has important implications for the governance challenge. The issue is compounded because there are two very different approaches to defining and living up to a corporate purpose. The first approach sees purpose as an integral part of leading and managing a large company. Purpose in this articulation is about where and how the company competes.

Purpose is what the firm is in business for, where it has chosen to excel and how, what behaviour is rewarded and what is not tolerated. Defining a meaningful and inspiring purpose is a key long-term CEO responsibility. The Lego example is instructive. Lego's widely studied purpose is:

"[T]o inspire and develop the builders of tomorrow."

Lego's story is a statement about concentrated attention as a governance priority. This purpose evolved to be at the centre of an overall architecture that includes key promises to children, Lego's people, its suppliers and other partners, and the planet.

Putting this purpose into effect took 10 years. What followed its conception was a re-organisation of the company to ensure that every aspect of the company lined up with this purpose. It meant getting back to basics, fulfilling orders in a timely manner and diluting Lego's interests in initiatives that didn't align with this mission. Purpose was pursued over profit.

From a company close to collapse in the early 2000s, Lego has become world leader in toys that children create from the ubiquitous 'Lego Bricks'. Lego was not always successful. The collapse in the early 2000s followed years of unfocused innovation, for example taking on the Japanese in electronic games. As Lego rebuilt its business to achieve leadership in interactive building play, its fortunes were fully restored – and then some.

What Lego and countless other purpose driven companies have proven is how a unified mission and vision that pursues purpose over profit leads to profit more often than not.

The second approach to purpose is quite different to the first. This approach sees purpose as the mechanism that balances and crystallises the usually diverse interests of stakeholders. This is called "stakeholder capitalism", in contrast to "shareholder capitalism" where shareholder interests come first. Following this second approach entails making trade-offs between the interests of five or so groups, with no single group having primacy of interest.

The emergence of B Corporations in the US where a company subscribes to an auditable set of non-financial objectives is an example of stakeholder capitalism. The US Business Roundtable's latest Statement on the Purpose of a Corporation argues that shareholder primacy should be replaced by the interests of five, presumably equal, stakeholder groups: customers, employees, suppliers, communities, and shareholders. The Davos Manifesto launched in 2020 added a sixth stakeholder, "society at large".

Investment funds with social purpose are making demands on the companies in which they invest that go beyond traditional investment returns. Similarly, in academic circles with the likes of Professor Colin Mayer of Oxford and in business journalism with the likes of Martin Wolf of the *Financial Times,* we see proposals to "rethink the purpose of the corporation" and an emerging literature arguing for stakeholder theory to replace shareholder theory.

Regulators and legislators are increasingly moving into this area. In the US, some 44 states have legislated to allow (but not require) directors to consider the interests of those other than shareholders. In Australia, a consultation draft of the fourth edition of ASX Corporate Governance Guidelines proposed that corporations not only were to act "ethically and responsibly" but also to act in a "socially responsible" manner. They also introduced the notion that companies have a "social licence to operate" and that Boards are therefore bound to take into consideration a wide range of social policy considerations.

These can include matters such as the human rights of the

employees of suppliers, paying employees a "living wage", offering employment to people with disability or from disadvantaged backgrounds, and responsibility for climate change in both a company's own activities and the use of its products by its customers.

While these guidelines have not been adopted, many influential commentators support the proposals, and many Boards are now grappling with the implications of these recommendations. These implications include developing an explanation of how to reconcile the often-divergent interests of five to six stakeholders. More specifically, who will adjudicate when different stakeholders do not agree with the Board's decisions? If the trade-off involves a non-economic decision, such as closing a plant important to a local community, what would stop a publicly listed company being taken over or resort to de-listing as a path for shareholders to obtain the economic benefit?

We note that polls of community sentiment overwhelmingly support corporations considering a broad range of issues when making business decisions. Conversely, current practice is held in low esteem by the general public. The vast majority of the community do not trust corporations to act in society's best interests.

However, adopting "stakeholder capitalism" with its reliance on voluntary undertakings by corporations to reduce externalities or deal with social problems is unlikely to be effective, and thus more liable to disappoint than delight shareholders and the community in general.

Trading off interests of five or six stakeholder groups is fraught with the danger of crystallising dissatisfaction. Who arbitrates conflicts, and how? In addition, the stakeholder trade off process further entrenches management who may skilfully use the potential for ambiguity and diverse views of different stakeholders to repel unwanted takeovers or otherwise further their own agendas. Journalist Steve Denning writes in *Forbes:*

> *"The fatal flaw in the 20th century stakeholder capitalism was that it offered unviable guidance on what is "true north" for a corporation. If big business attempts afresh to implement stakeholder capitalism, it seems likely to fail for this very reason.*
>
> *What's going on here? Cynics have concluded that stakeholder capitalism is nothing more than an elaborate public relations stunt espoused by big business to get through the current PR crisis. Business, they say, will go on doing what it has done since time immemorial: making money for itself.*
>
> *The attraction of stakeholder capitalism as a public stance is that it doesn't commit big business to do anything in particular. Firms can go on privately shovelling money to their shareholders and executives, while maintaining a public front of exquisite social sensitivity and exemplary altruism."*

The success of even prominent moves to adopt stakeholder capitalism is under scrutiny. In three articles published through the Harvard Law School Program on Corporate Governance, Professor Lucian Bebchuck and co-authors review stakeholderism, in their view typified by the Business Roundtable Statement on the Purpose of a Corporation. Among their conclusions is that stakeholderism is "an inadequate and substantially counterproductive approach to addressing stakeholder concerns". This research was published only one year after the Business Roundtable Statement, has been strenuously disputed by key figures behind the Business Roundtable Statement, and arguably comes too soon to assess the impact of that particular event. Yet this research suggests that the effectiveness of stakeholder capitalism is far from guaranteed.

This is not to deny that shareholder primacy doesn't have its problems. In particular, its timeframes are too short. The obsession with quarterly earnings permeates the ethos of too many companies. In addition, a sole focus on earnings ignores or underweights the interests of customers. Management consultant and author Peter Drucker described the creation of a customer as the only valid definition of business purpose. The new great firms – Amazon, Apple, Google and Microsoft for example – are all exemplars of customer-centric and purpose-driven firms.

A well-constructed purpose statement that is followed and observed can be an effective way to deal with public dissatisfaction. At less abstract levels, many companies are asking themselves whether they have a clear enough purpose to effectively engage with some combination of employees, customers and the community. The reasons for this "search for purpose" are many and complex. Many employees, particularly younger employees, need a clear purpose beyond a job to engage, and companies are in a race for talent. Customer engagement and brand now goes beyond the products and services supplied. There is a moral imperative for doing things for a greater good that benefits the company, its shareholders, customers, employees, or suppliers. Great companies, we are told, do all these things well.

The pressure is further compounded by the rapid emergence of external activists who pressure companies and directors on issues that have not traditionally been seen as part of their fiduciary responsibilities. These pressures are aimed at companies and often directly at Board members, for agendas that may not have anything to do with them directly but may play against their fiduciary responsibilities. These issues come in cycles. In recent years, examples include matters to do with climate change, marriage equality, refugees, and fair remuneration and working conditions. At the same time, activist shareholders are demanding the best possible economic returns. A company that does a good job of recognising broad purpose – but at a cost – is at risk of hostile takeover.

The argument that shareholder primacy is antithetical to other stakeholder interests is overly simplistic. In discussion after discussion with chairs and directors, it was clear that this choice generally arises when one takes a short-term view – a valid approach only in times of crisis. So, the notion that there is usually binary choice between shareholders and stakeholders is either flawed thinking or intentionally misleading. Conflicts between the interests of different stakeholders are not limited to economic returns versus the interests of other stakeholders. They include issues of employment in industries that are or are becoming incompatible with environmental standards or the environmental ambitions of the broader community.

Australian corporate law is quite clear that directors are able to take broader stakeholder interests into account and, unsurprisingly to anyone who sits around a Boardroom table, this is most often the case even though not every interest can be accommodated.

As Dr Simon Longstaff, executive director of The Ethics Centre, writes in *Ethics in the Boardroom*:

> *"[T]he practical reality is that directors are constantly being pressed to advance the interests of shareholders, as well as employees, customers, suppliers and the wider community. It would be comforting to think that all interests can be perfectly aligned – at least in the long term. However, that is mere 'wishful thinking'. The truth is that directors are frequently required to make decisions that will annoy one group or another."*
>
> *Consistent with the recent examples above, this framing places the issue of ethics firmly within the bounds of Board governance – and also frames stakeholder management and other topical concerns firmly as ethical issues. It also recognises the complexity of balancing these interests for the good of the company involved.*

What then is the Board's role in defining and watching over how "purpose" is to be handled, and how much Board time should this take? Unless there is time for substantive and thoughtful discussions around real trade-offs the firm faces, and how these trade-offs are put into practice, the search for and application of purpose becomes another box ticking exercise.

Defining a clear and meaningful purpose statement, one that can define how a company will move forward in a way that incorporates more than the financial, is now a necessary and helpful exercise for Boards. Forcing a focus on longer-term, broader issues can be a useful adjunct to and context for strategic discussions. Continual renewal of this purpose statement – including a clear description of why the chosen purpose fits with the circumstances of the company at a particular point in time – will be needed. Done well, it can give confidence that a firm's future direction has been given specific, tailored and intense consideration by the Board.

Similar concerns can be raised about other crucial board issues: culture, ethics, and non-financial risks. For example, as already discussed, ASIC's investigation into non-financial risks has identified a more-of-the-same approach as part of the problem. In culture and ethics, a process driven, tick the boxes approach won't make a difference. It would typically entail a report on culture often prepared with external help. The report will be brought to the Board, discussed, minuted and then on to the next item.

Reformers call for more time on these issues – for example, by deriding the CBA Board for spending only 10 minutes approving bonuses – but these critiques are themselves part of the more-of-the-same problem. The real remuneration issue in the Royal Commission proceedings was not the time spent but a failure to accept a more fundamental challenge: how to link pay to serious performance failures. Where is this extra time coming from, and what are the implications for the relationship between Board, CEO, and management? Boards do need to address the issue of purpose in light of the interests of multiple stakeholders. But doing this superficially in more-of-the-same mode is unlikely to be effective. Alternative approaches focussing on "best fit" rather than "best practice" need to be considered and are covered in the next chapter.

More-of-the-same can't drive meaningful change

A final and at times hidden problem with a more-of-the-same approach to governance is that it de-emphasises deeper thinking about actions that would materially improve governance.

The concept that increased boardroom diversity improves governance outcomes is now uncontested. Because increased diversity is linked to improved outcomes, and because of an acknowledgement that deliberate action is needed to overcome structural biases within current talent identification, development and recognition processes, setting targets and actions to increase diversity in senior roles is a major element of governance.

The ASX Corporate Governance Guidelines address diversity. They ask Boards to have and disclose a diversity policy, and to set targets and change management policies that will be reviewed with management and disclosed to investors.

None of this is controversial, but these requirements are a lagging indicator of what's needed, and what is being done and should be done, to drive improved diversity outcomes.

Diversity is, therefore, an example of an important structural flaw in more-of-the-same. A more-of-the-same approach is structurally biased to prescribe accepted elements of governance, even if this additional prescription is not based on any evidence. It can also not be relied on to identify and move to implement actions that are new or require path-breaking actions – even when evidence is clear.

The impact of more-of-the-same on governance failures

If more-of-the-same was likely to fix the four major governance failures outlined earlier, then we would expect that firms following these precepts would outperform non-compliant firms. Not only is this not the case, but the volumes of investigative work by Royal Commissions and regulators find governance failures even in leading firms.

How does adding areas of focus to the Board, increasing disclosure, retaining and extending mechanistic definitions of independence, and focussing on process, help?

This must be a central question in any discussion of more-of-the-same. Why should directors and chairs deploy the additional effort required to implement and then sustain the changes more-of-the-same implies if they do not contribute to improved governance performance in the areas of greatest impact and focus?

The biggest problem with more-of-the-same is perhaps not that any individual piece of guidance is poor, but that their cumulative effect is to move the focus of corporate governance discussions away from effectively meeting the most important challenges, and towards the achievement of worthy, but ultimately unsatisfactory standards.

We see little evidence or logic to support a view that more-of-the-same will make major governance failures less likely. The reason for this is not only that more-of-the-same lacks an evidence base, but that more-of-the-same does not address the causes of major governance failures.

The final chapters of this book explore ways in which governance failures might be better handled.

PART III

Equipping Boards to meet governance challenges

Our work so far has made two main points:

- First, there are serious governance failures, both in terms of poor business performance and falling foul of community ethical and legal standards.
- Second, the main elements of the proposed remedies have not worked and are unlikely to work in the future. We characterised this as more-of-the-same, the main elements of which are:
  - an emphasis on process versus outcomes;
  - a heightened focus on mechanistically defined director "independence";
  - director selection increasingly orientated towards technical competencies as described in a skills matrix;
  - increased disclosure to the Board and by the Board; and
  - loading the Board with additional conformance tasks in areas felt to be getting insufficient attention.

So, if more-of-the-same isn't the best way to handle governance failures, what is? This is the subject of the next three chapters.

We are mindful that black and white detailed prescriptions with universal application are unlikely to exist. In fact, putting forward any set of detailed, universal rules – which we would presumably assert would be so-called best practice – is likely to be another version of more-of-the-same.

As research on governance is largely inconclusive, our approach has been to draw on the practical insights of experienced directors as well as available research to argue for governance reforms that avoid more-of-the-same remedies. Because we reject the "one size fits all" approach, our approach is to identify broad themes that can be adapted to the different governance challenges Boards face.

Our first suggestion for improving governance is to jettison the notion of best practice. In its place we would substitute the idea of "best fit". This approach leads us to consider a range of alternative structures and processes to the best practice model, which is only one of a number of possible approaches.

In Chapter Six, we outline a range of other governance models. Each model is reviewed in terms of when and how the model best fits the challenge faced by the firm. Within broad parameters there is no "right" or "wrong" approach. Instead we discuss when and why the different approaches respond to the challenges of improving governance in a particular firm and at a particular time.

In summary, Chapter Six can be considered as a review of the architecture of governance, and how different architectures address different challenges.

With better fit architecture in place, the next issue, covered in Chapter Seven, is how a Board can more effectively operate in an era of increasing expectations as to what a Board should do in the time available. What are reasonable expectations, and what are unreasonable expectations. We propose Boards use two complementary approaches – focus and delegation.

Finally, Chapter Eight describes the vital role of the leadership of the Board chair as the integrator of these elements, and the individual who – given the shift in approach we are proposing – will have the flexibility and tools needed to better fulfil the accountabilities they already have.

Chapter Six

Best fit not best practice

In the field of management in general and leadership in particular, it is now well accepted that there is no such thing as universal best practice. The idea that there is one best way to lead and manage, such as Weber's theories of bureaucracy or Taylor's "scientific management" whereby the job of a front-line worker was analysed in terms of time and motion studies, has been discredited for more than 50 years. More recently, efforts to find a universal formula that distinguishes effective management and leadership, such as former McKinsey consultants Bob Waterman and Tom Peters' *In Search of Excellence* or their colleague and Stanford academic Jim Collins' *Good to Great*, haven't always withstood the test of time. The practices of the "excellent" companies that were claimed to underpin their success did not protect their performance reverting to the mean performance of their peer group.

Consequently, rather than seeking the holy grail of universal best practice, scholars and practitioners prefer to think in terms of what is called "contingency theory".

We contend that what applies well for management and leadership is equally applicable for corporate governance.

In this chapter we propose that rather than conduct a fruitless search for universal "best practice", Boards should seek "best fit" between the challenges they have and their resources, structure and processes. Application of contingency thinking to governance leads – in fact demands – this approach, a view I have held for many years.

Our focus is on applying contingency theory to the way Boards organise and equip themselves with the talent they need to contribute, in their specific context. This focus recognises that many governance challenges are problems with organisational performance, and that redesigning the organisational model is an important part of the solution. The tasks at which this talent should be directed are dealt with in Chapter Six.

Contingent on what?

The essence of contingency theory is captured simply by Stanford University organisational sociologist William Scott: "The best way to organise depends on the nature of the environment to which the organisation must relate."

Contingent governance approaches recognise organisations are open systems operating in fluid environments, and their effective management and governance needs to reflect the context in which they operate. The governance approach for a major financial institution operating in near-partnership with policy makers and regulators, has different demands from that of a resources company, just as a resources company has from a retailer, a manufacturer, a services firm or a technology start-up. Even within industries, companies face different contexts: rapid growth, deep restructuring, international expansion, regulatory or technological disruption.

The different roles of the chair in different companies highlights the difference between "best fit" and "best practice". On the one hand, a company may have a traditional governance structure, with a non-executive, independent Board presided over by a part-time, independent chair. Shares are widely held. Performance has been reasonable. This governance structure is contingent on the good fit between the governance model and the positive factors that distinguish the company.

Yet for another company, there may be a founder involved, with a significant shareholding, and a solid record of strong competent leadership. In this case a different "best fit" model would be appropriate. This model would accommodate the special case of the founder, accepting the founder as full-time executive chair and CEO. To do otherwise would not reflect reality: "even at a roundtable some people always seem able to sit at the head" to quote US cartoonist and author Ashleigh Brilliant.

Contingent choices are not made without substantial care, and not only because this approach is counter to more-of-the-same norms. Firms will wisely insist on examining carefully whether established governance patterns should be changed. Contingency thinking implies governance practices and processes should not be changed without good reason.

In the remainder of this chapter we examine five different governance models that could be used to help firms apply contingent thinking. These are:

- the ASX Board;
- an executive-heavy Board;
- the private equity model Board;
- the Governance 3.0 Board; and
- the two-tiered Board.

We examine these five models not as "the answer" to accommodate different situations. Rather we use the models to illustrate where a "best fit" approach might lead. Each of the models are described in general terms; in practice variations on these themes are possible and may be desirable.

For each variant we first outline what the model looks like in practice. We then identify the internal and external factors that drive the choice of each particular model.

Before discussing each model, we illustrate how contingency theory drives the choice of model. Two important contingency factors are:

- robustness of competition in the market where the firm competes – competition keeps managers on their toes as inefficient or unethical behaviour is punished by the market; and
- stability of the environment – disrupters require special focus.

The fit between these two factors and the models are summarised in Exhibit 2.

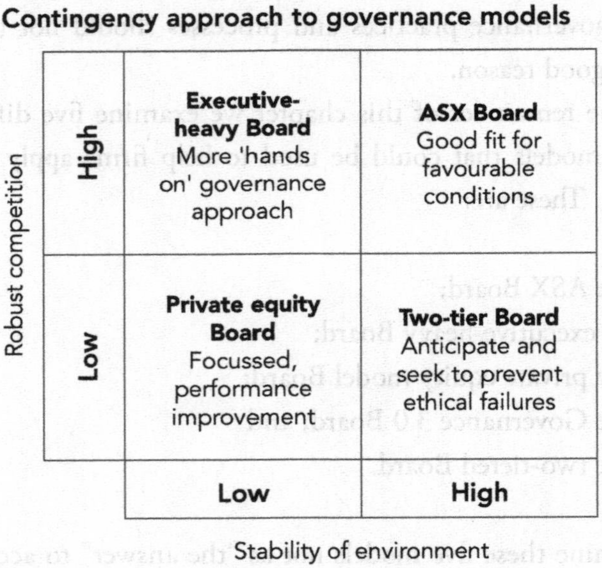
Contingency approach to governance models
Robust competition
High
Executive-heavy Board
More 'hands on' governance approach
ASX Board
Good fit for favourable conditions
Low
Private equity Board
Focussed, performance improvement
Two-tier Board
Anticipate and seek to prevent ethical failures
Low
High
Stability of environment

Exhibit 2

Each combination of contingency factors leads organisation designers to propose different governance models.

The ASX Board

There is a dominant governance model in the Australian listed sector: a single Board, comprised almost entirely of directors seen as "independent" according to ASX criteria, with a series of subcommittees targeted at specific compliance tasks. We refer to this model as the "ASX Board".

The essential features of this model are as follows.

There is a single Board of perhaps 10 to 15 members. These members are drawn from a range of backgrounds, typically a combination of former executives from other firms and professionals with backgrounds in law, accounting, banking, consulting or engineering. Many have multiple directorships, and often valuable and thriving interests outside corporate life. The vast majority of these are classified as independent by ASX criteria.

Directors receive significant remuneration. The Egan KMP report of 2018 shows top 50 companies' directors' fees of about $250,000 and fees for firms 51-100 of $180,000. That said, director fees even where a director serves on two Boards are often less than these individuals would have earned in prior or concurrent roles.

The Board typically meets about once a month, in normal circumstances. While monthly meetings are close to a norm, there is considerable flexibility about their duration – anywhere from several hours to two days. Committees – those dealing with crucial functions of audit, risk management and remuneration – also meet at least three or four times per year.

Special circumstances or events create the opportunity for additional discussions. Board strategy off-sites are the most common. Directors travel to a special location to spend two to three days discussing the firm's strategic direction often interspersed with visits to company facilities and meetings with staff. Corporate activity – purchases, sales or mergers and acquisitions (M&A) – as well as challenging financial or operational circumstances also receive additional time. As one of our interviewees remarked, in a crisis a director's time commitment is in practice almost unlimited.

Activity outside meetings varies, too. In some firms, access by directors to executives beyond Board meetings is strictly controlled. Elsewhere, directors routinely contact key executives asking for information or to convey views. Many conversations between directors occur outside formal meetings. Finally, as part of their personal networks, directors may gather informal intelligence from investors in their firm, or other stakeholders.

Even so, most of the formal information the ASX Board sees and seeks to base decisions on is provided or mediated by management. As with meeting frequency, director expectations of Board papers also vary. We have seen papers range from several page presentations to extensive, formal memos. (As in so many circumstances, there is typically no relationship between length and quality.) While some of these materials are provided by external experts, most are the outcome of intense effort and scrutiny by management before being released to the Board.

In terms of its operation, then, the ASX Board is in theory very flexible, and quite responsive to changes in circumstances once detected. The mechanism to provide this flexibility is the "if not then why not" principle. This allows departures from "best practice" to be explained, though as described above that is no guarantee of acceptance of the deviation by the ASX, shareholders or proxy advisers.

That said, the ASX Board designs-in a difficult challenge for directors: how can an organisation comprised of part-time, modestly incentivised individuals with information largely provided by management deliver appropriate governance to increasingly complex firms, including many of Australia's largest? Part of the answer is that this model can work well much of the time, for most firms.

At an industry level, two contingent characteristics define when an ASX Board will work well and when it won't. The first and most important contingent characteristic is healthy, active competition. Where competition is robust, market forces provide the incentive to management to operate and invest well. When managers fail to do so, competitors punish the company as they divert business away from the firm and to themselves. The prevalence of unethical practices in consumer finance raises questions about the intensity and adequacy of competition in these markets.

There is a second type of market competition that provides management with an additional incentive to perform effectively. This is the market for corporate control where shares are widely held, so a non-performing management will attract raiders.

In essence, competitive markets for products and services create performance and conduct discipline; they help do a significant part of the Board's work.

In competitive markets the governance model is less critical, and a vanilla product such as the ASX Board is adequate.

A second contingent characteristic is the stability of the environment in which the firm operates. In a stable environment with only occasional crises, the ASX Board can work effectively. However, substantial disruption is a challenge for the ASX Board.

Complete reinvention of corporate direction and purpose is rare in the listed company sector. We have previously described some of the challenges in conducting conversations about performance. Institutional barriers that frustrate this type of change include unwillingness for Boards and senior management to recognise and take action to support or combat disruptive change.

The ASX Board has limited opportunities for renewal or fundamental change. Removing directors and bringing in new blood is not easy, especially where there is no crisis. Unless there is a chair able and willing to reconstitute the Board, major change is unlikely.

Well established and understandable product and service offerings and customer relationships are also well matched to the ASX Board. Simpler products, or products that are used by customers with enough skill and history to understand them, reduce governance and conformance demands on the ASX Board. Similarly, to competitive industries, this type of product/customer pair designs-in resistance to behaviour that is, or could lead to, unethical conduct.

Finally, ASX Boards work well where it is possible to understand the firm's industry without great practical experience. Many Boards benefit from new to industry ideas and concepts. But other firms operate in industries where formally structured information needs to be combined with relevant practical experience to create the judgement upon which many Board decisions rely. Clearly, every ASX Board will have a mixture of backgrounds, but deep industry knowledge and history is becoming less common, and technical expertise with best practice compliance is becoming more common.

Even when deployed in the right contingent circumstances, the ASX model leaves firms exposed to all of the important governance failures and challenges we described earlier – in essence, this is the more-of-the-same organisation model.

In summary, the ASX Board model works best when demands on the Board are modest, and clustered around average conditions. This is not a criticism of the structure itself or those who serve on these Boards, but it is a statement about expectations and potential for impact. After all, most firms generate close to average returns most of the time.

That said, many of our most successful firms deploy highly functioning versions of this model to govern businesses that, for all their power and performance, fit the tests above.

Wesfarmers and Macquarie illustrate this point.

Wesfarmers model and basic strategy has been stable for some time, focussed on the intelligent if hard-nosed allocation of capital across a portfolio of loosely connected businesses. Most of those businesses have had simple products with clear and well established relationships with their customers. This does not mean that they are simple businesses, or that they do not require governing, but the nature and impact of mis-selling commodity or commodity like products, or fast moving and/or relatively low value consumer goods, is much less than for complex retail financial products. Wesfarmers has also benefitted from decades of focus on health and safety in the resources sector and in retail operations. Core risk processes have been well established.

Within a largely conventional model, Wesfarmers has departed from the ASX model somewhat in that there have been some prominent examples of transition from the executive team to the Board. A possible effect could be to ensure that the distinctive elements of the business model are preserved – a strategy that acts to make the ASX model more workable.

Macquarie also operates a successful, lasting ASX Board model. Like Wesfarmers, central aspects of its approach have remained constant, even as the nature of its activities has repeatedly transformed. Although some of its businesses do have more complex products or customer relationships, or are in sectors sometimes viewed as oligopolistic, in many cases these business units are relatively new entrants facing intense competition.

A particular feature of the Macquarie governance model has been the use of remuneration and consequence management as a method to prevent and in some cases punish ethical or performance failures. The Millionaire Factory is now a cliché, but for many years Macquarie was regarded as having effective incentive schemes that were part of a culture that attracted and rewarded talented executives.

More recently, Macquarie's former CEO Nicholas Moore's appearance at the Financial Services Royal Commission benefitted from the organisation's robust approach to detecting and removing executives who had exercised bad judgement or behaviour.

The executive-heavy Board

The ASX Board model can be extended by introducing directors with substantial direct links to the firm as current or previous executives or consultants.

Three variants are most common.

The first is the Executive Chair, typically a combination of the roles of CEO/MD and Chair. This arrangement is more common in the US than in Australia, and is commonly linked with companies where the founder or major shareholder has a strong and active presence. It is squarely opposed by the ASX principles, but reflects a reality that cannot be wished away.

The second is to retain an independent non-Executive Chair but to add one or more executives to the Board. This extends beyond the common appointment of a CEO to the Board, and often to the CFO, or at times a "Director of Operations" or equivalent.

The third is to retain former firm executives, or alternatively to re-hire former executives or consultants as Board members after some time away from the firm. If they join the Board before three years are up, they do not qualify as "independent" according to ASX criteria. We note there is no requirement in the ASX principles that all directors be independent – only a majority.

In all cases the overarching intent is to bring detailed knowledge of the firm and its industry to bear – knowledge that is unlikely to come from the outsiders who may otherwise serve on the Board. As directors, executives and former executives will also have detailed, fact-based views on strategic and performance issues that are or might come before the Board. Finally, an extensive directly relevant executive career is clearly a direct route to informed, experience-based judgements and a sense for where problems might lie.

The value of this inside information is highest in industries with complex regulatory conditions and industry dynamics. In these circumstances, the premium on detail gained through practical experience relative to the theory or the reporting Boards receive – even when it is of very high quality – is particularly valuable.

Retaining key executives may also be important in oligopolies with closely held industry knowledge. In these industries, potential new directors with relevant knowledge may have long relationships with the competitor. Past executives may be the best or possibly the only source of appropriate experience.

A related issue is talent preservation. The performance and capabilities of senior executives are well-known to the CEO and in many instances to directors. These capabilities can be demonstrated outside specific business silos: in many corporate organisations, executive leadership teams can form operating Boards where organisational peers discuss issues across a firm, or manage cross-functional activities. Performance in these forums can be seen as a useful test for performance as a director of the firm.

Other business characteristics also argue for executive-heavy Boards. For businesses that place a high value on a distinctive culture, executives as directors can bring a powerful instinct about what a business culture may mean, helping filter decisions and leadership behaviours.

Executives as directors can also provide additional continuity of business leadership, including the opportunity to find directors whose overall firm experience can match the likely timeframe of major strategic and investment decisions. For example, reflections about the origin and strategic and business logic of key initiatives from those who were there can be a valuable context in which to build on successes or to allow reflection about less successful ideas.

As with the ASX Board, these advantages come with watch points and risks that arise from the potential incentives and prior beliefs of key executives.

Probably the biggest, and most likely, risk is that the presence of past executives limits the introduction and discussion of alternative, newer perspectives on company performance and decisions. It can take considerable discipline for prior beliefs to take a back seat to new facts or circumstances. In addition, the possession of an enormous depth of knowledge, even if somewhat outdated, can be very influential.

There may also be an increased risk of can-kicking or other forms of deception. The detailed historic information past or current executives possess is a valuable source of intelligence on potential deceptive behaviour, but it can equally create motivations for past decisions, or indecisions, to be justified or sustained – even when circumstances are materially different.

A third watch point is the creation of an insider group of former and current executives – including executives not on the Board – and an outsider group of directors with no other experience at the firm. These groups can form because of aligned incentives including, for example, the defence of past decisions and judgements. They can also form because a shared, deep knowledge base encourages conversations in or outside of the Board that other directors find more difficult to share.

Box 6.1

Westfield Holdings – a pre-eminent example of an executive-heavy Board

- Executive, not independent chair
- Three or more directors were employees, or past employees and three had tenure as directors greater than 15 years
- Industry growth model – rent increases from shopping centres – hit a wall, a situation well understood by executive directors
- Board, led by the chair, effectively exited the business despite it earning attractive current returns
- Unlikely this would have occurred with an ASX model Board

Each of these watch points is the flip-side of the executive-heavy Board's key advantage – access to high quality and insightful information about an industry or firm. For companies that add executives to the Board, the judgement must be that these watch points can be appropriately managed, and the rewards for continuity of knowledge far outweighs the downsides.

The private equity model Board

If the executive-heavy Board adds additional current and past executive experience, the private equity investee company Board structure could be said to inject substantial, direct influence of investors.

The private equity Board model has been well studied, not least because the private equity business model – at the level of a private equity fund as well as an individual investee company – has developed a reputation for securing strong investor returns.

From a governance perspective, the Board of an investee company is the most relevant best fit candidate. The Board typically includes three types of directors: company executives, the PE firm portfolio managers who conceived of and executed the acquisition of the investee company, and representatives from the PE firm itself.

These three groups have different backgrounds but highly aligned incentives: they are all strongly incentivised to improve the performance and market value of the investee company. They may also be investors in the private equity fund itself, and so benefit from the performance of the investee company as well as gaining the reputational benefits strong performance will bring to the PE firm overall.

Some PE Boards also include a lead director. This director has the ability to allocate investee firm and PE firm resources for independent enquiry into operational, strategic and other issues. Like Netflix directors, PE Boards need not rely solely on information about the company to be provided by management.

A final structural difference is the direct and vital interest of the shareholder in management and Board activities. Some of this interest is expressed through the Board, and in other circumstances through direct conversations with management. This type of owner engagement is rare if not impossible for the ASX Board.

Operationally the model varies substantially from the ASX model. Smaller Boards, with more frequent and often ad hoc meetings, are common. This flexibility allows for fluid agendas, focussing mostly on performance but generally on issues that are perceived to be urgent as well as important.

This governance approach is tailored to the private equity business model. First, it rewards the identification and capture of performance improvement opportunities, whether identified in the investment thesis that underpinned the acquisition of the company or not. Second, aligned incentives also help drive co-ordination across the operational and the strategic. And third, the model goes to some lengths to align investors and management – in many cases by creating a substantial overlap within these groups and via remuneration.

This model is also important because it is designed to deliver outcomes that are superior to those put forward by alternative owners, including the previous management and Board, and in many cases rival acquirers in a competitive process. The recent auction for Virgin Australia is an example: rival firms competed on the basis of multi-dimensional business plans for a business of national significance that impacts multiple stakeholder groups.

This model has proven adaptable to more complex businesses and more complicated stakeholder environments. This is by necessity: in the US companies have raised more money in private markets than public markets every year since 2009, and private and public firms alike have risen in size and complexity. In addition, private-to-private transactions are increasingly common, allowing liquidity events for management or funding of growth in ways that previously required public markets.

The PE model is also associated with outperformance compared to the listed company sector. Multiple studies suggest PE returns are higher and less volatile than for public companies, although these results come with the associated suspicion that PE managers can exert a degree of control over when and how assets are marked to market, or that additional financial and operational risk are being taken.

The challenge this model poses to the ASX Board is: if directors with more time, more information and more incentive to act are more able to scrutinise and improve management actions, why is this not usual practice?

The contingent circumstances that argue for this Board arrangement are those under which the private equity business model is typically focussed. In broad terms, these are:

- Variability in firm performance. Private equity turnaround opportunities are richest in industries where variation of firm performance is high, suggesting ample performance improvement opportunities. There may also be the potential to create a high performing challenger firm that can, for some time, exploit the strategic umbrella provided by large underperforming incumbents.

- An active, fluid industry environment with multiple organic and inorganic growth opportunities. The private equity model is designed to deliver outcomes that are superior to those put forward by alternative owners – that is, to succeed in the market for corporate control.
- A relatively simple regulatory environment. The private equity Board model is tilted to performance. While this doesn't imply non-compliance with legal or ethical standards, the incentives and inclination of those involved are likely to be more focussed and engaged on driving increased performance than on managing complex stakeholder and regulatory environments.

The private equity governance style is, in theory and based on our interviews, set up to seek to capture performance opportunities through a combination of disciplined management and focussed risk taking.

Why is this more achievable within a private-equity style governance environment? A major reason is the combination of strong incentives and direct experience in commercial risk-taking and judgements on the Board. Like the executive-heavy Board, the private equity Board is equipped with additional deep business knowledge through the presence of management and portfolio managers who did the deal. Lead directors and senior PE firm figures also bring risk-taking expertise. With these skills around the Boardroom, a focus on performance improvement can naturally follow – along with a number of potential blind spots.

Another lens on this problem is to understand how the private equity model extends the ASX and executive-heavy model. Like the executive-heavy model, a higher proportion of directors have direct operational experience in the business, deepening the availability of information, albeit from a single source. Beyond direct management experience, PE-style Boards prioritise experience and capabilities that are directly relevant, developed either as active investors generally or in the industry concerned. Compared to the ASX Board, there is less room for the professional director, and less room again for the professional director with experience in professional services and other less immediately relevant fields.

The risks of this model arise from the challenges of translating a shorter-term governance model into a permanent option. It would be surprising if the private equity model – designed to drive actual performance or create performance potential in a shorter horizon – rolled naturally into a lasting governance approach. Conventional wisdom is that a private equity investee company may be in a portfolio for perhaps five years.

The most natural risk introduced by this background is that the Board's focus on performance results in insufficient scrutiny – over time – of longer term issues. Can a typically activist PE-style Board adapt to discussions about longer-term strategic shifts, or multiple phase strategic responses? Retaining institutional memory can be a challenge for traditional Boards, and the presence of executives on the PE Board is likely to address this. Instead, this challenge is more of temperament and focus.

Similarly, is this model going to allocate sufficient time to properly address complex conformance and ethical issues? Real world experience is that private equity-owned companies comply with ethical and legal requirements. That said, as discussed above, although this model is adaptable to different contexts its presence in the most complex stakeholder environments is less common.

Private equity-style governance is present in the listed sector. The many examples include firms such as Premier Investments, where an activist founder remains as a major shareholder and Chair, and works closely with a CEO focussed on growth and financial performance as well as business unit accountability.

Governance 3.0

An emerging model of governance is a deliberate attempt to introduce some of the ideas behind the private equity model to the listed sector.

This model, described as Governance 3.0, is intended to equip some key directors on the Board with more information, and more time, to provide additional scrutiny of and challenges to management, and be in a position to transmit the benefits of this scrutiny to investors.

The model is that of a traditional ASX Board but with a small number of more empowered directors. These directors – two or three, but by no means a majority of the Board – would be different in four important ways:

- have substantial, differentiated incentives more closely linked to firm performance, and at a level consistent with their additional time requirements and accountability;
- an expectation of a full-time or near full-time role;
- access to an independent support staff, independent advisers and direct access to management and data; and
- be limited to short terms (three or five years), to reduce the chances of being seen as de facto management.

These more empowered directors would have several advantages for management as well as to shareholders. First, greater available time and independent information gathering resources can avoid information asymmetries common in other models. Second, empowered directors may be able to become more credible with institutional investors who cannot always receive a full understanding of competitive strategies in traditional market briefings. Finally, and most obviously, these directors can deploy personal time and firm resources to address complex performance and business failure issues even if typical Board agendas are crowded with a range of less important matters.

Empowered directors could also play a role in scrutinising the audit process and findings. For example, one empowered director could be effectively full time on audit. While deliberate concealment by management is rare, it is often not picked up via traditional audit.

The additional horsepower this model provides is of most value when industry and business circumstances are intensely competitive and dynamic. The logic behind this model is that under these conditions, directors limited by traditional Board roles are unable to provide appropriate scrutiny of either performance or conformance.

Suitably skilled directors are hard to find in these industries, and in many cases are likely to have multiple options – some of which are likely to be more attractive financially and even in terms of role and freedom to act.

At an industry level, fluid technological and regulatory contexts also argue for this model. These conditions further increase the value of directors with practical experience.

Governance 3.0 is also designed for high complexity businesses. Multiple businesses and/or products, risky or high consequence customer relationships, and a product or service suite that places a premium on high ethical standards all constitute signals to adopt this model.

Strategic complexity is also a sign to move to this model. Boards that are faced with a very uncertain set of choices, or without a dominant choice, may value the second opinion a group of empowered directors can provide.

Finally, a related benefit could be in flexibility and speed to adapt. While empowered directors are able to provide additional scrutiny, once a direction is chosen, then empowered directors can provide additional horsepower to speed change, increasing the ability of an organisation to adapt to fluid industry circumstances.

This model's distinctive design choices drive the risks and watch points.

The simplest and most obvious negative is that this model may require a substantial increase in the direct cost of governance. Director fees would increase, and stronger incentives would push up against conventional wisdom of how director incentives should reflect the interests of shareholders, particularly minorities. Governance 3.0 would attract significant attention for this reason alone.

A second potential downside is that the presence of these empowered directors depowers and demotivates management. The additional involvement and freedom inherent in the Governance 3.0 model increases the chance directors will begin to manage the business in a meaningful way. Even if this doesn't happen, the empowered directors will be asked to equip the Board with independent and presumably divergent views on business performance; a contest of ideas that – if it becomes unbalanced – reduces the actual and perceived confidence in management by the Board.

A related risk is of much more upwards delegation, for either quite honest or perhaps more cynical reasons. In the former case, it may make sense for management to respond to apparent Board signals to prefer to call on the views of the empowered directors in certain areas; why should management give these areas previous levels of effort? In the more cynical case, management could seek to deluge the Board with data on relatively routine matters to absorb this additional horsepower.

To our knowledge, this emerging model has not yet been implemented. But it is being seen as a credible, emerging option by governance experts, and the appeal as a next-generation solution for an increasingly complex business environment is clear.

The two-tier Board

In other geographies, the issue of managing substantial complexity has been addressed through the two-tier Board. In Germany, it is the predominant governance model – the equivalent of the ASX Board in Australia.

The essential design of this model is that a supervisory Board has the right to appoint – by election among the supervisory Board members – and to remove members of the management Board, and that in turn the supervisory Board is appointed by a combination of employees and shareholders. The supervisory Board can also determine the remuneration of the management Board members.

This system seeks to create a very clear division between the making of business decisions – from the day-to-day to strategies and capital allocation – and their review. The mandatory presence of employees on supervisory Boards also makes it a requirement that decisions take more than shareholders into account in reviewing decisions.

The apparent promise of this system is that Boards offer a combination of the time and skills needed to protect the interests of investors in businesses that have many other critical stakeholders – including those with very complex needs.

In practice, the lived experience in Germany, for example, does not always bear this out. Like the ASX Board, the historic context of this governance model arises not solely from a concern about stakeholder values, but other factors including the relative role of debt and equity, the influence of unions and employees, and the nature of minority protections for shareholders. Consequently, it should not be a surprise that the supervisory Board does not always fulfil the more contemporary duty of complex stakeholder management.

It is also apparent that the two-tier Board does not prevent major governance failures. Volkswagen's supervisory Board could not prevent its Dieselgate problems. Wirecard's supervisory Board did not prevent its collapse or the criminal conduct of key executives. Views of the model also wax and wane with the German economy.

The supervisory Board is said to suffer problems that may also be identified in the ASX Board. The first is that supervisory Board members are captured by management, or lack the information and time to properly supervise and review management decisions.

Contingency theory suggests that two-tier Boards may have a place in Australian corporate governance, but that these Boards will need to be designed to cope with a specific set of current governance challenges, not by adapting a model that was developed in a different time and place.

These circumstances include the presence of multiple stakeholders with complex and perhaps contradictory objectives. Rising organisational complexity, including the number and complexity of relationships with customers involving sophisticated products, is one circumstance – this covers many of the challenges identified in the financial services sector. Banking and wealth management, and the fiduciary duties that these businesses often imply, are clear and contemporary examples. A range of companies have found the conflicts between business value and customer outcomes difficult to manage.

A second sign is an industry structure, particularly in relation to levels of competition, that makes poor conduct less likely to be scrutinised through competitive pressures. As a business strategy, established customer franchises, barriers to customer switching, and complex products that make the purchase decision complex and unattractive to review, can appear attractive. But any strategic gains from these characteristics will be short-lived if they are allowed to dull an organisation's sense of fair dealing and ethics, or if they are allowed to become permanent substitutes for strategic development.

A final circumstance is the need to accommodate interactions with regulators that are increasingly complex and to some degree collaborative. This is perhaps a new governance challenge, or one that has not been sufficiently recognised until now. It is a readily acknowledged challenge to detect and monitor poor outcomes, or to manage consequences of those outcomes in terms of new policy or executive remuneration or tenure. That said, there are now legitimate conformance duties that involve the review of business methods even in the apparent and perhaps actual absence of poor outcomes. This is inevitably placing new demands on Boards' conformance functions.

The invitation that arises from these contingencies is to frame a two-tier Board model that creates distinct groups focussed on performance and conformance. This could include a management Board similar to the current ASX Board, but reporting to a supervisory Board with specific expertise and accountability for risk management and review.

This two-tier structure would give additional time and space to discuss complex conformance problems. This Board structure recognises that – even with the best available approaches – some organisations inevitably require large amounts of time to identify, help resolve and decide ongoing policy responses to conformance issues. It also reflects that this time and space is especially valuable when conformance issues have major and perhaps immediate impacts on business value.

This structure also improves accountability at the Board level of conformance issues. Even as management teams have expanded the role of Chief Risk Officers, and have sought to improve executive accountability for conformance failures, there have been few similar structural changes at Board level. This structure makes clearer which Board members are the conformance specialists, and those who are focussed on the performance side.

Finally, it could invite the increased, and more focussed, contribution of a growing group of risk and conformance-oriented directors who, our interviews suggest, are not as well suited to discussions about corporate performance.

The two-tiered Board comes with a number of watch points. Like the Governance 3.0 model, there would be a substantial increase in the cost of governance, and (albeit in a different way) the complexity of Board operations. Although manageable at the margin, these increases make more challenging the recruitment of a sufficient number of talented directors, and the management of dynamics within the Boardroom.

There is also evidence that the two-tier Board – particularly in the supervisory Board – can attract yes-people captured by management. This is a common criticism of the German two-tier experience; even moving to an Australian variant may encourage a rubber stamp approach to conformance monitoring.

Finally, any new tier will remain (in the absence of any other changes) reliant on the information provided by management, the time available to consider key issues, and the skills and personal characteristics of the directors on both Boards.

How can decisions about Board structures be made?

Contingent changes to the essential structure of Boards and governance practices promise major disruption as well as substantial improvements in effectiveness. Choices to move from a broadly understood and supported model suffer from the bias against many innovations: whether to select a certain but possibly suboptimal outcome or to exert extra effort at the chance of a better result.

To be effective, any change will also require the support of shareholders. At the simplest level, governance is for shareholders – they should be given the opportunity to influence how it is performed. But more fundamentally, any new model will take time to implement, refine and prove up. Shareholder approval will be needed to give management and Boards the breathing space for this to happen.

These imperatives mean any application of contingency theory should be based on clear signals about the potential to permanently improve current governance performance, and a process that engages shareholders in a genuine conversation about governance – one that offers potential rewards far in excess of the current forms of shareholder democracy.

Shareholders should be vitally interested in the outcomes of a contingent approach to governance design – and so decisions to move to any new model attract appropriate attention.

A discussion of contingent options should be welcomed by shareholders. Opportunities for shareholders to meaningfully engage in governance matters are limited, and focussed mostly on reactive crisis management. As discussed previously, major governance failures – if and when detected – are increasingly seen by shareholders as deserving of immediate consequences. CEO and chair positions are under increasing scrutiny – but arguably this type of shareholder engagement with governance is mostly retrospective and leads to improved governance indirectly, if at all.

A step in the right direction might be for the ASX Corporate Governance Council to acknowledge that companies should have Board structures so they are "fit for purpose" and encourage models different from the guidelines providing they are strongly articulated.

Other opportunities for shareholders to participate in governance discussions are either in private, heavily mediated by proxy advisers, or AGM-orientated set-pieces that are about governance only indirectly.

Increasingly, shareholders use the remuneration report as a proxy for satisfaction about management and Board performance: management performance through rejecting remuneration advice; and Board performance by rejecting the Board's judgement about the proposal's acceptability. At the same time, however, few shareholders seek the immediate removal of specific directors – itself probably a statement about the need to improve governance through a Board's collective performance.

A discussion about alternative governance models is an opportunity to increase the quality of this conversation, including by focussing the conversation on proactive improvements, not only on extracting consequences for previous errors.

A sensible starting point would be that the adoption of a new governance model should be an explicit choice approved by two thirds or 75 per cent of shareholders.

These are similar supermajorities to those needed to approve other major changes to company constitutions, or to major corporate arrangements. This change is and should be substantively different to the creation of a new Board committee, or the appointment of a single new director, or other incremental changes to governance approaches.

A supermajority is needed to protect the interests of minorities – this is a common reason for supermajorities in other contexts.

It is also needed, however, to ensure that shareholders with interests in governance improvements are given opportunities to contribute.

Chapter Seven

Focus and delegation

In this chapter we argue that two mutually reinforcing ideas – focus and delegation – offer a practical theme in the search for improved corporate governance. Too easily dismissed as motherhood, these concepts can help directors cope with the reality of overly full Board agendas.

These two ideas are complements. Focus without effective delegation is impossible. Delegation without focus is abdication. Together they allow a Board to govern effectively, drawing on the expertise and experience of directors on matters of substance. In this chapter we first discuss why to focus, where to focus and how to focus, and then review some examples of delegation.

Why focus?

Focus is crucial to successful management and leadership strategies. Focus recognises that no organisation can do everything in the very best way. Hence focussing on the set of activities where the organisation can have the greatest positive impact on its competitive position is key.

> **Perspectives on focus**
>
> Microsoft co-founder Bill Gates: "My success, part of it certainly, is that I have focussed on a few things."
>
> Apple co-founder Steve Jobs: "People think focus means saying "yes" to the thing you've got to focus on. But that's not what it means at all. It means saying "no" to the hundred other good ideas that there are."

Likewise for Boards and leadership teams. Not every issue is of equal importance at any one time. A key challenge of leadership is to know when to focus or not to focus on particular issues.

There is a story about a prestigious UK institution which had just recruited a new director. The new director asked the chairman what were the key items listed in the notice of meeting. "Oh," the chairman replied, "these items in your Board papers are merely window dressing. In my view there is only one serious agenda item at every one of our meetings. That is to test whether the Board continues to have confidence in the CEO."

While this anecdote is arguably overly simplistic, it is a clear statement of that Board's focus and priorities at a particular time. Boards intuitively understand the importance of focussing on matters that are important and where the Board can have impact. For example, it is widely understood that CEO appointment or removal is a critical decision that only the Board can take.

Formal governance advice seems to be the opposite of focus. Regulators, exchanges and industry bodies keep broadening the role of, and demands on, the Board in an attempt to ensure nothing can go wrong. The implicit assumption is that most matters are of equal importance most of the time.

Some of this advice has come from a misinterpretation of recent governance concerns. Many of the concerns raised since the GFC, and in Australia since the Hayne Royal Commission, were the responsibility of the CEO and their top team. It is CEOs, not Boards, who determine culture, though the Board has an important role in promulgating ethical behaviour. It is the CEO who must strike the right balance between long-term and short-term focus. It is the CEO who brings the Board into the strategy process as a constructive partner. It is the CEO who makes the key recommendations on remuneration. The board should and must delegate these and other responsibilities to management, otherwise they themselves become management.

Focus is a necessary response to demands to broaden attention. Expecting a Board to take on substantial additional duties as well as pre-existing core roles requires increased focus on what matters most. Focus matters because, no matter how much time a Board has available, there is an impossibly long list of issues on which the Board could be asked to provide guidance or approve a decision.

Contingency theory can guide focus, just as it can guide Board structure and processes. Rather than a generic list of expanding areas of focus, a contingency view seeks to identify the matters that are key to a particular Board operating in particular circumstances at a particular time. Though a list such as this is hardly controversial, the key question is which issue demands the greater focus at any one point in time?

To illustrate, appointments of the CEO, chair and directors may be critical if the Board is plagued by turnover of key people when what is needed is stability and support. Alternatively, the appointment of a new CEO with an outstanding record of long-term business building takes CEO appointment off the table, until dealt with when succession is addressed or when unexpected issues with respect to leadership arise.

To work through their list of potential areas of focus, Boards must decide what the most critical functions are at this time, what level of scrutiny and involvement it is reasonable to provide, and how the any additional areas can best be handled.

When this challenge is not met, monthly Board meetings and annual Board meeting cycles get filled with standing items, crowding out the capacity to increase the effort on more important but more difficult issues that may not even be on this list. This implicit and even unrecognised deprioritisation process leaves directors open to accusations of neglect when failures in these areas emerge, which can be damaging even if not life-threatening.

Determining focus is not only a practical compromise to handle additional responsibilities. It also needs to be recognised as a primary driver of Board effectiveness. The question is where Board focus and involvement is of most value. It is all too easy for a Board to become enmeshed in reviewing an operational risk or a risk/return trade-off. Decisions to rationalise manufacturing facilities, or automate customer service, should balance multiple factors: improved returns, impacts on quality of customer service, and local economic impacts. There is no question directors can assist in evaluating or reviewing such trade-offs, but how often will this extra effort have impact? In many cases, the Board's role should focus on whether management is making these trade-offs in the best way, rather than sharing responsibility for day-to-day decisions that flow from practice or policy.

Improved focus is superior to more time

The Board's functions are often classified as those central to either:

- performance: achieving the required shareholder returns to underpin the long-term support of investors; or
- conformance: ensuring the alignment of management and shareholder interests, and that the company operates ethically

and within the relevant legal frameworks.

Strictly Boardroom argued the key focus of governance should be to ensure management is continuously striving for above average performance taking account of risk.

In the ensuing period, most of the increase in workload on Boards was on compliance and risk – driving further demands on conformance versus performance. Consequently, as discussed in Chapter Two, progress in both areas has been modest.

This lack of progress suggests more time – particularly more time spent on compliance – is not helping. Most of the failings that have surfaced in the current governance crisis are in fact direct failures of compliance – for example failures to observe the six principles outlined in Commissioner Hayne's report – that have occurred despite time spent on compliance matters, which by all reports has increased considerably.

This has one of two possible implications, that either:

1. the extra time spent on compliance is still not enough; or
2. the time spent on compliance is not as effective as it could and should be.

We opt for the second explanation, and conclude that yet again increasing the time spent on the same (or even new more detailed variants) of conformance activities by non-executive directors is not the answer.

No matter what the area, demanding more time of directors is a solution that may be approaching its limits within the ASX Board model. People with the skills and experiences to be effective directors are in short supply, and increasing the time needed to do the job further reduces the available talent pool. Moreover, having directors spend significantly more time on their role blurs the line between governance and management. If this happens, a new set of governance issues emerge, firms will have trouble retaining top executive talent, and decision making will become slower, more ponderous and more risk averse.

Boards who determine for themselves that more time is the only answer should consider alternative governance approaches.

Where to focus and what to delegate

To avoid fragmenting available time across broadening agendas, Boards should act deliberately in allocating their increasingly scarce available time, delegating to support or enable this focus.

Which areas of focus are most likely to make the Board more effective? Two principles can help answer this question:

1. Boards must, by definition, focus on matters that cannot be delegated to management or subcommittees. These include:
    a. key personnel issues: specifically, CEO appointment and removal, Board and chair appointments and removal, and executive remuneration
    b. capital allocation, including major investments and divestments; and
    c. oversight of risk and financial controls, including audit outcome.
2. Boards should focus on matters that have the potential to put the firm and its sustainable performance at risk. Examples include expanding offshore or entering a new market that doesn't fit well with the core business (for example wealth management and consumer banking or food retailing and hardware); betting early and big on a new technology; or tolerating irregularity and ethical non-compliance
3. Boards should apply contingency thinking to identify the

matters that could put the firm at risk. This requires judgement about impact, but also creativity and discipline to contemplate issues management may not want to discuss. How does one determine, in advance, whether a matter – particularly an unusual event – may cause material damage to the firm?

Based on our conversations, three common areas that meet this test are:

1. approval of the overall corporate strategy and purpose, without which the direction and performance of the firm can be put at serious risk;
2. acceptance of risk policies and periodic review of their application; and
3. acceptance of specific hole below the waterline risks that are judged by management to require Board sign-off.

Beyond these matters, the Board should seek to delegate most other matters, including more of their routine compliance work, to management, who in turn are supported by external expertise as appropriate.

How to focus

In the balance of this chapter, we will discuss some processes that help Boards focus, and then delegate, to give time back while enhancing appropriate separation between management and Board.

As the best focus is contingent, this discussion must be somewhat high level. For example, a focus on CEO effectiveness and fit is more useful if couched in terms of the leadership issues the Board decides to focus on at the time. Has the firm been losing executives it would have liked to keep? What do senior executives really think about remuneration discussions? Do shareholders respect the management and Board? Do management's perspectives and answers to Board queries hold up in the face of Board examination?

There is no set process for determining focus. Typically focus emerges from robust and honest discussions on performance. Discussion is aided by the chair posing some key questions. For example:

- What are the three areas of our activities that worry you most? Why?
- Where and when are our deliberations going nowhere?
- How do our people stack up versus key competitors?
- If we could close or sell one part of our business, which one and why?
- If we could add a new business to our portfolio, what areas should we explore?
- Where are we under-investing and where are we over-investing?
- How does our investment strategy compare with that of our leading competitors?

These questions have a common theme: while directors should not be across operational details, there is real value in having an informed sense of how a company – and the Board – is performing against areas critical to long-term success.

Questions like these are often best handled by each director writing brief answers, then sharing answers, and then discussing the different viewpoints that have emerged.

The natural leader of this process is the Board chair. However, an outside facilitator is often useful, allowing the chair to participate fully without the burden of managing a meeting that can and should expose key opportunities and vulnerabilities, and different points of view. Clear information, such as a quantitative model of the economics of the firm, can also point the Board to where to focus.

Delegation's role in support of focus

Effective delegation is an essential enabler of focus. Delegation is not abdication of responsibility. It is an essential element of management theory and a long-established practice since the invention of the large corporation or indeed any form of significant institution.

Delegation is particularly necessary in detailed compliance-related activities. No-one we interviewed argued against reducing the compliance burden on Boards. But since the GFC and Hayne Royal Commission, hoping for simpler and less onerous compliance is unrealistic. Effective delegation is therefore of central importance in the areas of detailed compliance-related activities if Boards are to have any hope of discharging their overall duties effectively.

For example, the APRA/CBA Review highlighted weakness at the CBA in handling "operational risk". These operational failures led to failures to report cash transactions. In an organisation of the size and complexity of the CBA, it beggars belief that a part-time director could know where to prod to identify and evaluate such a risk. The executives designing and reviewing IT systems have the best chance of finding and framing operational risk. But, as the Boeing 737 MAX disaster shows, even in an area as critical as aircraft safety to an aircraft manufacturer, operational risk from IT failures was not discovered in time. Expecting the Board to have a full understanding of operational risk is unrealistic. If the situation is complex and specialised, calling in outside professionals is likely to be more effective than having, say, an IT specialist on the Board.

In corporate governance, delegation is typically undertaken via key committees in the areas of audit, risk and remuneration. These established arrangements provide clues about how delegation can be better applied.

Audit provides a good example of the balancing of focus and delegation. The goal of the committee is well established and understood – to provide an accurate, timely and relevant picture of the accounts. The audit committee is generally chaired by an independent director and comprises a clear majority of independent directors plus occasionally an outsider not a main Board director. Typically, much of the work underpinning the responsibilities of the audit committee is delegated to the chief finance officer (CFO) and external auditor who jointly manage the audit process and take the committee through a draft set of accounts. Once questions are raised and resolved the report goes to the full Board with a recommendation to approve. There is generally little discussion unless controversial items or decisions are recommended. Directors rely on the auditor and CFO to highlight the key issues and in particular to highlight decisions "close to the line of acceptable accounting". By and large audit committees work well although even this is not without its critics; the performance of the audit process is currently under heightened scrutiny not only in Australia (in the form of a formal parliamentary review) but also, notably, in the UK.

Audit is strengthened in many companies by the appointment of an effective internal auditor. The internal auditor has a direct line to the CEO, and is expected to raise and escalate matters that should be of concern.

In contrast to audit, the objective of the risk committee is unclear, even as its intended scope increases. The committee is clearly responsible for both financial and non-financial risk, mainly operational risks as described earlier. Identifying and putting in place measures to mitigate the risk to the extent feasible is largely a subjective, judgemental process. Often serious risks aren't foreseen and, sometimes even when identified can't really be managed away. Covid-19 is the best and most recent example. Directors we interviewed believed

Covid-19 highlighted a concern that obvious risks are increasingly being microscopically managed, while big risks such as pandemics, disruptive technology, another financial crisis, or international tensions creating trade barriers, receive inadequate attention.

A broader role for the risk committee may create the impression that risk can be managed out – in other words, that if a bad event occurs, the Board has failed. This is incorrect, and not based on any sound understanding of risk management. Risks can be minimised or mitigated but not completely prevented. More so, business is all about intelligently accepting risk. Firms that better manage the balance between risk and return outperform. Investors can choose the potential of higher returns that expose them to more risk.

Indeed, there must be a question about why Boards have felt the need to establish risk committees, and indeed for management to create chief risk officers. The most obvious explanation is that Boards are dissatisfied with the quality of management's ability to perform the task we describe above – that is, to identify and address risk in their decision-making. To this extent, the rise of the risk committee is another type of performance challenge.

The remuneration committee also has an important role, but its usefulness has declined as the disclosure requirements of the annual remuneration report, and the use of a vote on it as a mechanism of general protest, has tied those participating in this process into increasingly unproductive endeavours.

Effective delegation

What do these committees and their practices say about the proper design and functioning of a delegation process?

Many corporations are building a top team of executives who can support the Board and committees in handling audit, risk and remuneration. If not carefully designed, the executive compliance process delegates up, producing more paper for the directors who oversee these functions. This is not a theoretical point. There are many observed examples of management simply transferring risk or burying committees in voluminous detail rather than exercising genuine delegated responsibility. However, with strong leadership from the Board and CEO, compliance executives can relieve much of the Board's burden.

Our proposition of focus supported by delegation goes well beyond saying, for example, "management should lead on operational risk".

Effective delegation is precise. It identifies:

- Who has line responsibility for the delegated matter, or is to be held responsible?
- What key activities does the Board expect the delegate(s) to carry out?
- What standard of performance is expected?
- What time frames for key milestones must be observed?
- When does an issue have to be reported up?

For example, a delegation of operational risk would cover:

- Responsibilities of the chief operating office and direct reports.
- Key activities would be to discuss and document the areas most likely to become problems, and carry out specific reviews triggered by, for example, a rolling review schedule, a complaint, unusual turnover of staff or shareholder voice.
- The expected standard of performance and time frames for significant issues to be reported to the risk committee chair is 24 hours from identification, and for the report to include recommended remedial action.

How might this approach work for the new areas of concern, namely purpose and stakeholder interests, culture and ethics? These areas are integral parts of the CEO's role, and the CEO should be prepared to discuss these topics on an annual basis, or if specific issues raise concerns. An appreciation by the Board of culture and ethics is rarely helped by a glossy document with all the standard phrases; effective delegation processes go far beyond that. Insights on how to design new and robust delegated processes can be drawn from other areas where this is already well developed, audit and safety being two examples.

Focus and delegation in practice

Three familiar examples illustrate how focus and delegation can work in practice: CEO appointment, CEO evaluation and company strategy.

The first two of these cannot be delegated; in the third the temptation if anything is for Boards to under-delegate through overestimating their ability to add distinctive value.

CEO appointment

Appointing a CEO and monitoring how the CEO leads the company and deeply understands its business, as discussed earlier, is a key area of focus for the Board and one where delegation is difficult.

What makes this a challenging area? Experience suggests one serious challenge is to detect within the background of an experienced, very accomplished executive any personality traits that are likely to be destructive to the functioning of the firm and its ability to attract and retain top people. The most common dangerous traits are narcissism, hubris and sociopathy. As business development specialist Eric Jackson described in his *Forbes* article "Why Narcissistic CEOs Kill Their Companies:[61]

> *"...narcissism in the executive suite can be expected to have effects on substantive organizational outcomes, potentially including strategic grandiosity and submissive top management teams. Narcissism can affect an executive's choices in such areas as strategy, structure, and staffing."*

While the narcissist frames all issues and decisions around themselves, a CEO suffering from hubris is overconfident and fails to see difficulties in proposed courses of action. A CEO with a sociopathic bent will damage morale, lose good people, and often creates an environment of fear – recall the discussion of Theranos earlier.

There are three reasons why Boards have trouble identifying these damaging traits.

First, many signs that a potential CEO suffers from narcissism, hubris or sociopathy are often well hidden, and in moderation these traits are seen as positive. A narcissist will come across as confident, energetic and articulate. The underlying narcissism only appears later, when the CEO's concern with image, and refusal to see mistakes, leads to poor decisions and investments. Narcissism can be misunderstood as confidence and a positive approach. Similarly, a sociopath can present as a "no nonsense" manager focussed on the job. Only later is it apparent that good people are leaving the firm.

Second, the processes followed in appointing a CEO are often flawed. One-on-one interviews with the Board and senior management are, in our view, key. Reference checking is becoming harder because of legal issues, but is still vital, especially when undertaken by the chair and other directors.

Third, because the chair will work most closely with the CEO, the chair's view is often not challenged sufficiently when the candidate is being interviewed and discussed. If a chair, after being challenged, says, "I hear you, but I believe I can work with the candidate and eliminate your concerns", directors feel they can't push back harder and useful dialogue can be short changed.

Usually the Board is assisted by a search firm. A useful contribution of these firms can be clarifying what the Board is looking for in a CEO. But delegating the interviewing and assessment is likely to be a mistake. Outsourcing reference checking is at best a supplement. If outsourced, it should be considered whether it is best undertaken by specialists rather than the search firm involved in the appointment.

The point is well covered in a *Harvard Business Review* article "Don't hire the wrong CEO".[62] To quote:

> *"Given the importance of appointing a CEO, it is puzzling to us that Boards are so willing to delegate the search to outside firms. Clearly, Boards should use professional advice wherever appropriate. And, in fact, many head-hunters are careful, thoughtful, and highly qualified to help in many aspects of a CEO search. But our experience shows that the most responsible Boards keep control of a CEO search, carefully directing the activities of the search firm, using it as staff and as additional eyes and ears – and as an independent sounding board – but never as a decision maker.*
>
> *Basically, search firms do what they are told to do. And that is fine, as long as they are told to do the right thing. If a Board confuses general management skills with genuine leadership, so will the search firm. If the Board develops a narrow, technical profile for a position, the search firm will take the description literally and try to fill it with someone who has exactly those experiences and responsibilities. In essence, head hunters look to fill round holes with round pegs."*

CEO evaluation

Boards, led by their chair, have a critical role in evaluating the CEO's past and potential future performance.

CEO evaluation occurs in two different ways. One is the formal processes such as Board members providing views to the chair at the chair's request. Input from subordinates may also be sought, for example by a 360 degree review. Another formal process is a meeting of non-executive directors to discuss how they believe the CEO is travelling. This is also supplemented by discussions involving only directors, including the CEO.

Second are informal processes. How does the CEO relate to the top team? Is the CEO respected? In particular, Board discussions on strategy or management depth and succession are shaped by the way the discussion provides insight into CEO performance. Directors are looking for high quality explanations of what is happening in the markets in which the firm competes and how the CEO sets a fine-tuned strategy. They are particularly concerned to see that the past statements of what the company is doing, and expected results, turned out to be largely true, or if not, satisfactorily explained. They are also wary when unanticipated surprises seem to catch the company off balance. Directors can also make judgements about the effectiveness of management by observing how senior managers reporting to the CEO perform in Board meetings and/or in informal conversations around site visits.

For evaluation to be useful, it should have consequences. These include feedback, preferably constructive. The most serious consequence is dismissal. It is also the most difficult matter to deal with. A chair we interviewed described how easy it is to get off track in evaluating a CEO. Directors had concerns, but were providing relatively bland feedback to the chair who they believed supported the CEO. The chair mentioned his surprise at the evaluation, as he had serious concerns about the CEO. Directors then expressed relief, as they thought the chair wanted to keep the CEO. Once the misunderstanding was cleared up a decision to terminate the CEO appointment was readily made.

Another confounding factor in evaluating the CEO is company politics and often long-standing personal relationships. One eminent chair explained the need to be careful and objective, and not to be misled due to a personal relationship with the CEO.

Data on CEO tenure suggests Boards are increasingly using the appointment and dismissal of the CEO as a key lever in providing oversight. According to the recruitment firm Robert Half, their 'CEO Tracker' showed 63 per cent of ASX top 200 CEO's have been in their role less than five years, 25 per cent have tenure of six to 10 years and 12 per cent have tenure of 11 years or greater. Tenure of CEOs in Australia and in major overseas markets has been steadily declining.[63] One study reported at a Harvard Law School governance forum found median CEO tenure in the US has dropped from six years in 2013 to five years in 2017.[64]

This declining tenure suggests Boards are struggling with the challenge of both selection and performance management of CEOs. Excluding the (rare) circumstances where CEOs are appointed to do a job with a finite deadline, repeatedly resorting to dismissal can be a sign of poor Board, not CEO, performance.

Boards can gain considerable insight into CEO performance from discussions on the performance agenda including strategy, succession, and key personnel issues for the top team. In contrast, the conformance agenda tends to be dominated by Board members strong in finance and risk, and provides little insight into the effectiveness of management in leading and running the businesses. As conformance eats into the time available for strategy and personnel issues it is no surprise that the Board's judgements on the CEO take longer and are less clear-cut.

In terms of focus and delegation, evaluation of the CEO is unarguably a primary focus of the Board and, like CEO selection, has few appropriate options for delegation, other than some supporting activities discussed above. This is important context for the overall demands on the Board as the time needed for this genuinely distinct Board role must not be crowded out by competing demands that may be more readily and appropriately delegated.

Company strategy

Approving strategy is an example of a widely accepted responsibility of the Board. While CEO appointment and dismissal is always a key role requiring sharp focus, when asked what other areas deserve strong focus, the most common answer is "strategy".

But what is meant by strategy, and what is the most constructive role a Board can play? There are two common answers to this question. One argues that the best role for a Board is to review and, if appropriate, approve a strategy. What the Board sees is largely a well-developed and considered product.

An alternative is for the Board to participate in the development of the strategy through workshops, discussions, expert presentations, and strategy retreats. Under this option, the Board has a more direct input into the strategy and exposure to data and other relevant materials.

We prefer the first approach – review and if appropriate approve strategy – precisely because this is a delegable process and is arguably more effectively the work of management rather than the Board. A key reason for this, beyond the considerable demand it can put on the Board, is because the dynamics of a Board/management co-development process make it difficult to achieve a productive outcome. Directors don't want to be shown up as asking dumb questions. Management can be reluctant to tackle directors who have different views or important critiques but who at the same time decide on their tenure, promotion and pay. What is intended as an open, no-holds-barred discussion can rapidly revert to guarded, PowerPoint dominated presentations with little true dialogue. Both Board and management are disappointed, and the corporate strategy is rarely improved.

The review and approve role does not have these problems, or at least not to the same extent. Management advocates a strategy to which they are committed; the Board tests this by questioning, with the expectation that, done well, the strategy will be approved, or more work will be carried out on specific areas of concern.

This is a good example of where the Board can deploy effective delegation and focus on their critical contribution; to review and access the strategy brought before them rather than being integral to its development. Developing a coherent and impactful strategy is a considerable task that is unlikely to be the best use of a Board's scarce time availability. This is because the real strategy of the firm is reflected in its decisions, actions and progress towards an agreed goal, and not just in a polished document. Rather than being involved in cascading the strategy into individual decisions, the Board is much better placed to deploy its collective and diverse experience to stress-test key assumptions, seek evidence for key choices and consider critical risks. For example, many strategy documents will include "customer centricity" as a key element of their strategy. Yet the treatment of customers, as has been recently witnessed in the finance sector, is often quite different to the intent. Similarly, many firms whose strategy rests on being "low-cost producers" can lack comparative analysis of their cost base, or have failed to realise significant savings year after year.

The Board is the last stop for evaluation of strategic choices which are rarely appropriate to share publicly. A Board is better placed to delegate strategy development to management and their advisers and focus their efforts on its evaluation. This does not exclude a level of interaction between Board and management in the process. But the focus of that interaction is best, we believe, when the roles of each party are clear and understood.

The exceptions to this general approach, and consistent with the idea that contingent thinking should guide a Board in these decisions, is where the Board judges there is need for a serious intervention in the strategy development process. Perhaps as a symptom of a different problem, even then, such a role is likely to be at best a transient focus rather than a permanent characteristic of the Board's role.

Deliberative agenda setting is needed

Precisely because Boards effectively have the right to go where they want, they need to be highly disciplined. Focus and delegation become two essential sides of the same coin when it comes to practically navigating the realities of Board governance today.

Without greater attention to where it focuses and where it should delegate, uniform application of governance guidelines can lead a Board to being safe but non-distinctive, normative rather than fit-for-purpose. The wide range of circumstances and challenges faced by ASX 100 companies simply cannot be best managed without deliberative prioritisation by the Board, and only the Board itself can do this. Equally, those providing guidance and regulation on Boards need to be acutely aware that this is a key to good governance and provide Boards with the mechanisms to enable effective focus and delegation, rather than constrain them in increasingly uniform approaches.

Given the wide range of businesses operating across the top 100 listed companies, we would expect to see more, not less, variance in how Boards choose to organise themselves, where they focus their major attentions, and how they delegate effectively to ensure high quality governance outcomes.

Chapter Eight

Leading the Board – the chair's contribution to governance

Achieving best fit structure and processes that provide the Board with appropriate and necessary focus and delegation won't "just happen". Nor will these aims be achieved by further regulation, especially when regulation increasingly predominately relies on a one-size-fits-all approach. In our view, what it will take to improve the effectiveness of governance is action by the Board, through the leadership of the chair.

In almost every aspect of management, effective leadership makes a substantial difference and the leadership of Boards by chairs should be no exception. And yet, relative to its absolute importance, and also compared to the attention rightly paid to CEO appointments, the process of the appointment of chairs is disproportionally under-examined.

Our search of the literature and our interviews suggest the contribution of the chair in governance is not given enough attention. In our interviews the selection of the chair and the chair's role in leading the Board were unambiguously raised as a key issue, and at times the key issue, underpinning high quality governance. It was put to us that if only one change in governance was possible, that change should be to elevate the role, talent, recognition and efficacy of chairs.

The chair is in a strong position to create and maintain a constructive dialogue about how best to organise and operate the Board in the context of its environment and membership. Put another way: if the chair can't tackle these issues, who can?

Chairs should also be strong drivers of company performance. As with the Board, the role of the chair can be framed as having focus on assuring process quality and risk. In practice, however, the decisions a chair makes may be as important as many operational decisions. These decisions include errors of omission, where Boards are allowed to defer more difficult questions.

A company's behaviour in crisis situations is another sign of the importance of chairs. Many of our interviews took place in the early stages of the Covid-19 pandemic. Compelled by these circumstances, directors we interviewed recognised that chairs and Boards generally had roles in adapting governance processes to deal with immediate, important issues. These included difficult judgements about remedial or at times business-saving actions, and in later stages judgements about how to appropriately deal with furloughed employees, or accepting payments such as JobKeeper when earnings and dividends were maintained or at times increased. Merger and Acquisition environments also call on chairs to manage difficult communications and often lead and/or strongly influence negotiating positions.

The chair's leadership contributions extend beyond the Board to senior executives. High performing CEOs are likely to choose firms with high performing chairs, and over time high performing Board and CEO leadership aids in the attraction and retention of other high performing executives. While some tension between Boards and executives is expected, Board governance that is ineffectual or unhelpful can lead to departures of CEOs and other senior executives.

While there are many excellent chairs providing sharp focus and good governance, there is actually little guidance available to chairs beyond broad statements of intent and as in other areas of governance, no rigorous research. Chairs who want to contribute to addressing the governance failures outlined in Chapters One and Two are unlikely to find much of the available literature of practical use.

Many discussions about Board leadership focus on skills, processes and personal qualities. These discussions extend to compliance and legal issues, and typical "director's duties". They may also include discussions of achieving productive group dynamics, or of appropriate and effective methods of conducting board meetings. Information and advice about these issues is widely available. More recently there have been recommendations to provide in situ advice through the mandating of psychologists into the Boardroom and management meetings.

Implicit in this view is that if a Board has the right meeting management and interpersonal skills, and is able to work together in a constructive way, this will be enough to create and achieve high governance and firm performance.

Put another way, meeting management and interpersonal skills may be necessary but are not sufficient to ensure the Board is dealing with the right issues in the most constructive way.

This chapter explores the importance of the chair in the context of our "best fit" approach. The essence of the best fit approach is to reflect the particular situation that chairs face, not set standardised approaches. It proposes actions to increase the quality of leadership of Boards by chairs and hence the effectiveness of their roles. It examines seven issues that, when addressed, will help chairs be more effective drivers of Board and firm performance. These are:

- more rigorous selection of chairs;
- improving the role clarity of the chair;

- choosing the right directors;
- skills of an effective chair;
- the chair's role in providing the Board with relevant, high quality information;
- developing a nose for potential trouble; and
- setting the pace and ambition of change from the chair.

More rigorous selection

The importance of chair selection is self-evident, yet directors and chairs we spoke with readily identify shortcomings in current practice.

In conversations with directors, notwithstanding the presence of many excellent chairs, the shortcomings in how chairs are chosen was routinely raised. Observations ranged from current appointment processes for the chair being too "political" at one end of the spectrum to placing too much emphasis on "who wants to be chair", as opposed to "who should be chair", at the other. The problems with navigating this process extend beyond the Board table with one senior head-hunter noting that the characteristics of a good chair are, even for experts, difficult to clearly define. Adding to this complexity is that no-one wants conscripts in the role and, as is often the case in leadership, the best leaders are often reluctant to take on the chairmanship, as they appreciate the responsibility and complexity of the role.

When the appointment of a new chair is being considered, a typical process is for a senior director who is not a candidate for chair to speak one-on-one to each director asking:

- Are you a candidate for the chair, and if so what would you bring to the role?
- If not, who should be considered and how should we go about selecting and appointing a new chair?

It is usual in this approach for one or more directors to put their hands up. The choice process can become quite political, as when the notion of "it's my turn" or "I am best for this role" competes with that of "colleagues don't support you" or "there are better candidates not on the Board", or "we need an external intervention".

Many Boards have a deputy chair who often has expectations of taking the chair when the current incumbent leaves. When the company is not doing well the stakes are often higher and hopefully the politicisation diminishes and a search focuses on finding the best candidate, with clear air in which to operate. This appeared to have happened following the Royal Commission, which triggered a number of new chair appointments.

The weakness in chair selection processes is perhaps symptomatic of an underlying risk of the chair being seen as an obligation that needs to be met, a reward for years of service, or a position of status and recognition; not as a pivotal role, with requisite skill and personal attribute requirements.

Clarity on the role of the chair

Variable selection, and unclear guidance about what a chair should do, can result in widely varying views on the role of the chair. Broadly characterised, the range of these roles can be described as:

- First among equals: as observed through language such as "is it then the Board's wish…?"
- Custodian of good governance: as observed through language such as "we collectively need to spend more time linking strategy and remuneration"
- Partner with and counsellor to the CEO: as observed through language such as "the CEO and I believe we should…"
- Efficient meeting manager: as observed through language such

as "we have a full schedule today and need to stop discussion of item X at this point." Or "I would like to move on and now draw your attention to P6 of the CEO's report".

In practice, combinations of these characterised roles can also be found, for example "partner with and counsellor to the CEO" plus "efficient meeting manager".

In our view, there is inadequate discussion to assist a chair in knowing how to best carry out their role in the specific context of a particular company at a particular time in the evolution of that company and its industry. This is not a simple discussion where simple rules can be invented to be applied uniformly. It is also difficult to do from a distance as not everything a chair is dealing with is observable from a distance. Nonetheless, meaningful discussion about the role of the chair is important and demands more attention.

In the past few years some helpful thought pieces on the chair's role have been published. Most recently, Justice Jonathan Beach in *ASIC vs Mitchell (No 2)* put forward a role description reflecting his view of community expectations of the chair. Consistent with our observations, a summarising practice note from commercial law firm Corrs Chambers Westgarth noted that Justice Beach found little relevant guidance in either case law or the ASX's Corporate Governance Principles[65]. Justice Beach's helpful contribution to the description of the chair's role was summarised by Corrs Chambers Westgarth as:

- While the Chair is not a 'directorial overlord' and does not have authority to manage the corporation, he or she does have the power and authority to manage Board meetings and so may have greater responsibility for the performance of the Board as a whole.
- The Chair has responsibility for setting the agenda for Board

meetings and must ensure that the Board has before it sufficient information to consider, discuss and decide on the agenda items. The Chair is responsible for ensuring the Board has sufficient time to attend to necessary matters.

- The Chair is responsible for ensuring "workable and harmonious relations" between executive and non-executive directors and between the Board and executive management. The Chair must also manage unhelpfully disruptive directors.
- The Chair may have greater responsibility for ensuring that the Board sets and implements an appropriate corporate culture and corporate governance structure within the organisation.
- The Chair must ensure appropriate communication with and the taking into consideration of the interests and concerns of members of the organisation.
- The Chair may have a public relations role in respect of the Board and outside parties.

Justice Beach's comments provide a valuable generic role guide for a chair. This role confirms to some extent the view of a chair as one who co-ordinates activities without deciding. There is a sense that the chair has a special role in ensuring the best quality decisions can be made. We discuss how this can be done in more detail below.

Justice Beach's comments are silent on one key issue. That is the chair's role in navigating the appropriateness of the current directors individually, and as a group, to provide effective governance. Removal of directors is not easy, and is technically a shareholder decision, not a chair or Board decision. However, in practice the chair has an important role and considerable influence in how to deal with non-performing directors, or diversity or competency gaps, via direct, private conversations. With three-year terms for directors, the most common way for a chair to deal with Board dysfunction or gaps arising from the mix of directors is to not support reappointments; a timeframe that is not always ideal.

Corrs' practice note goes on to comment that:

> *"If it was ever in doubt in modern corporate Australia, [this case] clearly establishes that the role of the Chair is not merely ceremonial. All directors should carefully consider whether the Board skill matrix properly records their special skills and experience, with Chairs, in particular, noting that they may one day be held to a higher standard as a result of these professed talents."*

Another perspective is provided by a major survey and interview program from the European Business School, INSEAD, which was summarised well in a 2018 *Harvard Business Review* article by INSEAD Professor Stanislav Shekshnia.[66] His research sharply differentiates the chair's role from the CEO's role, while acknowledging that because many chairs are former CEOs, this differentiation can be difficult to sustain in practice. The article reports that the INSEAD research had distilled the requirements for the chair's role down to eight key principles:

1. Be the guide on the side; show restraint and leave room for others. Keep chairs' "air time" below 10 per cent of meeting time.
2. Practise teaming – not team building. The Board is not a team – it is a coming together infrequently of a group with disparate skills interests and commitments.
3. Own the prep work; a big part of the job is preparing the Board's agenda and briefings.
4. Take committees seriously; most of the Board's work is done in them.

5. Remain impartial.
6. Measure the Board's effectiveness by its inputs, not its outputs. Quality of people, the agenda, the data and briefing papers.
7. Don't be the CEO's boss.
8. Be a representative with shareholders, not a player.

Meeting all these criteria all the time is rare, but our observation is that good chairs follow these guidelines most of the time. While many executives need to shift gears and mindsets to follow these, successful chairs say the effort pays off.

The commentaries reflect the perspective that the role of the chair can often be more precisely and more formally defined. But it also highlights the importance of appropriate constraints on the exercise of management power, and the consequent importance of focus on the setup and functioning of the Board itself.

Because the Board appoints and approves remuneration of the CEO, and because the chair has a major say on these issues, the chair has potentially great power over the CEO. This is even more the case when the chair is the founder of the company or has long experience and involvement with the business. Justice Beach recognised this risk, cautioning that the chair is not a "dictatorial overlord" and does not manage the company, a point reinforced by the European research. The implication is that while the chair has potential power, there are problems if it is used in a way that makes the chair de facto CEO. These circumstances can cause many strong CEOs to leave, and even if not, have the potential for confused decision making.

The chair/CEO relationship is critical to effective functioning of the Board. The relationship should be built on trust and respect, with differences worked through amicably and collegially.

Perhaps with this reason in mind, many CEOs carefully monitor, and in many cases insist, on highly controlled direct interactions between directors and their executive team. In addition, many directors we spoke to are very alert to the risks of being placed, de facto, in the role of management. Even in special circumstances, for example in temporary emergency structures created to manage impacts of Covid-19, directors we spoke to were very conscious of not performing management's roles.

In summary, the Board chair is not a "boss" of the company or CEO as it is often misunderstood to be. The chair's authority flows from effective leadership and functioning of the Board. As Professor Stanislav Shekshnia describes it: good chairs "understand that the Board is the collective 'boss' of the CEO and that the task of the chair is to make sure the Board provides the goals, resources, rules and accountability the CEO needs". A chair can be an effective counsel to the CEO, but not direct the CEO.

Nor is the chair a team leader as they are often misunderstood to be. As INSEAD research pointed out, a Board is not a team that works intensively together but is rather a group exercising independent judgements periodically, and particularly in the face of major decisions or crises. We would suggest rather than the team analogy for Boards a more useful one to help understand their role and leadership is that of a group of judges led by a Chief Justice. Each judge brings an independent perspective which can lead to split decisions or dissents as well as unanimous decisions. The Chief Justice may at times be in the minority but this doesn't imply a failure of leadership. Instead, what is going on is a process where people with specific knowledge, skills and experience come together relatively infrequently to probe and make judgements about the performance and direction of the corporate entity or with respect to specific issues where a decision is needed.

Choosing directors

While directors are ultimately appointed by the shareholders, there is no question Boards exercise considerable influence on the choice of directors. Investors expect Boards to indicate which candidates they endorse. As leader of the Board, chairs therefore have a responsibility to ensure such endorsement is well considered.

While the CEO appointment is the Board's most critical personnel decision, high quality governance also requires the chair to be focussed on enabling the appropriate appointment and removal of directors.

We have discussed already the limitations of the skills matrix approach that is part of the more-of-the-same approach to governance. Like so many other governance improvements, a skills matrix is insufficient to guide director choice; the best that can be said is that a skills matrix is a signpost to a successful process – one that should be led by the chair.

This type of individual leadership, and the judgement that comes with it, is necessary to improve Board quality. For example, while gender diversity on Boards remains a difficult challenge, individual leadership can make a difference in the recruitment of women in a way that will be less constrained than waiting for the usual selection processes to unfold.

Research by proxy adviser Ownership Matters[67] found there is a strong bias toward appointing existing ASX300 directors to vacancies (in pool appointments). Strong individual leadership is needed to break away from this notion of the 'directors' club' model of selection and towards one that recognises performance outcomes.

We have dealt with corporate performance as a governance issue already and, again, the chair's leadership of the Board in ensuring company performance is important. The Ownership Matters research links performance to director choice, finding that "Non-executive director (NED) tenure is lengthy and that board turnover during the last 15 years is largely independent of company performance." They conclude there is a pool of ASX300 directors who are not appointed on the basis of company performance and then go on to ask: "If a high-performance culture does not exist in the Board, investors should ask how one can prosper within the company's domain?"

How should a chair respond to the challenges posed by these established patterns?

The formal process for appointing new directors is via the nomination committee. Increasingly, companies turn to executive search firms to identify and vet potential candidates. Arguably the most critical issue in appointing new directors is building the genuine diversity of skill and capability needed to access and use all available talent, and to avoid group think. Here the chair plays a critical role, not only in leading the selection of directors but also in effectively bringing new directors into Board discussions.

Removing a director is a less visible and somewhat more mysterious process. The legal framework is clear – shareholders appoint new directors and do not re-elect, or vote to dismiss, existing directors who have lost the Board's support. There are two very different core reasons for a director leaving a Board (other than by natural retirement or through other reasons of self-selection). One is the director is judged to be unable to contribute effectively to the Board process for a variety of possible reasons. The other is the changing nature of the company's situation requiring a shift in director mix, and so otherwise strongly contributing directors need to give way for contributors who satisfy different needs.

Removing an underperforming director is the more difficult of the two and is typically handled via one-on-one meetings between the chair and the director who has lost support. While no chair enjoys this process, it requires strong leadership and has the benefit of sending a strong signal that directors are expected to either contribute effectively or leave the Board. These are never easy conversations, which is why director removal is more often handled by not nominating a candidate for re-election once a term (typically three years) has expired. Depending on a director's remaining tenure, overreliance on this approach can obviously be suboptimal.

Key skills of the chair

It is generally recognised that effective leadership requires a blend of hard skills such as setting an agenda or interrogating financial reports that come to the Board, and soft skills evidenced by effective interpersonal relationships. Our observations highlight the importance of both types of skills in the chair's leadership of the Board. The type of hard skills we have in mind include:

- Setting and holding to an agenda that reflects the focus required of and agreed to by the Board.
- Ensuring the composition of the Board is up to the key tasks facing the Board via Board and director reviews and appraisals.
- Ensuring the Board is properly informed to make the decisions it is facing, including not being overwhelmed with detail nor starved of vital data or perspectives.

Soft skills include:

- Creating tough, honest, harmonious and constructive discussions.
- Deliberative handling of performance and succession for directors and the CEO.
- Building partner-like rapport with the CEO while maintaining a clear separation of roles.
- Sensitivity to values and culture issues.
- Effective communication with stakeholders.

These skills are not the same as those required to be a high-performing director. Their requirement arises from the distinctive role of the chair as the leader of the Board and not the company.

This role also suggests a different set of performance criteria and therefore skills for chairs as distinct from fellow directors and CEOs. Directors we spoke to suggested increased scrutiny of the performance of the chair is better defined in terms of how well the chair is setting the agenda, ensuring necessary information is provided, and in leading constructive, collegial though hard-nosed discussions. It was also argued that chairs need sufficient experience to be able to exercise judgement on difficult subjects, see where problems are potentially emerging, and assess whether the company is being well led. There is a role here for Board and director evaluation either by a committee of the Board or an independent outsider.

Providing high-quality information

As described in Chapter Four, a more-of-the-same approach mistakenly assumes that governance can be improved through the availability of more, and more detailed, information to Boards.

Most directors identify this resulting information overload as a problem working against effective governance rather than a source of improvement. In the short term, it contributes little to informed decision-making; in the longer term it erodes the attraction of being a director and so reduces the director talent pool.

Perhaps unusually, this frustration occurs at a time when pressure on Boards to be better informed is increasing. The Financial Services Royal Commission identified a series of incidents that arguably Boards should have been aware of. In retrospect, these examples are part of a broader wave of new things that Boards are expected to be across. For example, most merger and acquisition activity now includes due diligence that encompasses a range of Environmental, Social and

Governance matters, as well as traditional commercial issues.

It is the chair's job to ensure the Board receives the information it needs. This includes but extends well beyond the vital but initial step of ensuring materials are manageable. The topic of information quality, as opposed to length, seems to have been largely ignored in much of the current discussion on Board governance and yet in both our interviews and our own professional experience this is a major weakness.

Securing high quality information for directors is critical as it addresses directly a number of governance challenges that arise from Boards being unaware of poor business performance, bad corporate behaviour, or weak risk controls. Irrespective of how skilled the directors of a Board may be, systematically providing poor quality information to their decision making can only reduce their effectiveness. While chairs are clearly not responsible for preparing the information provided to the Board, they are in a unique position to set the standard and determine what is acceptable and what is not.

In doing this the chair is often making choices between materials internally managed, mediated and prepared, and those from external sources. While no external observer can or should be able to replicate the granularity of information available to management in an environment where governance failures can be caused by misleading behaviour by management, external input is one helpful antidote. On the performance side, external perspectives on business, financial and operational performance can also be helpful antidotes to the risk of internal group-think; at a minimum they can be useful perspectives to push against in discussion.

Insights relevant to each stakeholder group pose different challenges to secure the most accurate and appropriate information on the issues relevant to that group. That said, one general perspective is that stakeholder information that comes heavily mediated by management is of less value than direct channels. Experienced chairs recognise this and manage for it by reviewing how information on issues relevant to each major stakeholder group is best brought into the Board's information flow.

Business performance information

Surprisingly, a deep, well-structured history of business performance and its drivers are often a missing ingredient in the information going to the Board. Long-term performance and returns provide a guide to market conditions, particularly the existence of cycles in business performance, or longer-term pressures on margins. Current performance provides better insight when compared to past performance and the reasons for changes are understood.

This information should be easy to prepare, but our experience is that many businesses don't have an agreed picture of their own history and its underlying drivers. Being bound by historic performance is rarely wise, but historic performance can help to identify business units, including newer ventures, that are beginning to perform more strongly as the future moves closer. Just as important is the ability to link long-term financial history to physical and market-related drivers of performance. Even in rapidly changing industries, Boards – particularly in a period where new directors are joining – that link financial and business drivers help build an understanding of past and future performance.

Similarly, information that objectively and critically provides comparative performance and its causes is also very helpful and too often absent from Board's information sets. Relative to internal performance, insightful comparative performance is relatively rare and often reserved for annual strategy sessions and even then, is usually under-considered.

Employee-related information

Views of employees with respect to values and culture are commonly sought. Many leading firms have culture surveys that disclose whether employee matters are getting better or worse. There is a limit to the usefulness of these surveys as management has major input into design and interpretation. Nevertheless such surveys can reveal areas of potential concern.

Investor-related information

Information from investors is one example where structured, direct, widespread engagement is valuable. CEOs and senior managers operate highly structured internal employee engagement programs including "town hall" meetings and one-on-one discussions that span organisational levels. By contrast, investor interactions can be seen as "tasks to be managed".

A striking feature of our interview program was the reported lack of direct shareholder interaction between individual independent directors and shareholders. Many directors reported that when shareholders want information, they speak to management. Investors we spoke to agree this is typical.[68] This is not surprising, as usually investors and analysts are after forward-looking detailed information. Similarly, investor road shows are usually handled by investor relations professionals and the CEO and CFO. Although directors from some of our larger companies reported more widespread engagement – for example, extending beyond AGM season – this was by no means a universal view. It was surprising that many companies had limited regular structured interaction between investors and the directors, especially when one considers that directors are in effect acting on behalf of shareholders.

While large investors are quick to make the point that "if we need to speak to the chair or Board we know we can", there is arguably too little attention given to proactive engagement by the chair (and directors) with investors. Where there are examples of this, such as the type of investor listening tour that would often accompany a CEO appointment process, one director we spoke to was quick to emphasise how unusual and helpful this was for those directors who were involved.

(Our interviews also suggested that investor engagement processes risked a skew to larger shareholders through ease of engagement and an increased need for support. Although probably not as troublesome as insufficient engagement, there is a risk here that – for example – smaller investors with divergent and perhaps challenging views are crowded out of the Board dialogue.)

This observation about the challenge of securing meaningful input from investors into the Board process sits in contrast to the ASX Corporate Governance Guidelines which say that a "listed entity should have an investor relationship program that facilitates effective two-way communication with investors". That said, the framing of this guidance is not directed at creating a direct connection between directors and shareholders. Other jurisdictions place a stronger emphasis on this. The UK Corporate Governance Code, in contrast, makes it clear that "engaging with shareholders – and wider stakeholders – is an integral part of a Board's leadership role". The UK Code highlights this and suggests the chair – and other senior directors – have specific responsibilities:

> *"The Chair should also ensure the Board has a clear understanding of shareholders' views. Non-executive directors should be offered the opportunity to attend scheduled meetings with shareholders and expect to attend meetings if requested by major shareholders. Senior independent directors should attend sufficient meetings with a range of major shareholders to listen to their views in order to help develop a balanced understanding of the issues and concerns of major shareholders."*

In the US and Canada, leading Canadian governance expert David Beatty reports that:

> *"[A]s a direct consequence of shareholder activism Boards and executives frequently review lists of the largest shareholders in order of percentage of holdings. They then decide on a consultation strategy that may well include a visit from an independent director without any management being present."*[69]

Beatty identifies this type of engagement as important because:

> *"[Boards] that don't understand alternative points of view on corporate strategy or bring them to the top management team for consideration can never be fully confident that the management's view of the world is the right one."*[70]

Because of the likelihood the chair will have a more active role with investors/shareholders, the chair holds a particularly influential role in determining how to forcefully deliver investor insights to the Board.

Customer-related information

Many customer research efforts fail to provide genuine insight due to the simple fact that this research is difficult and the research question often poorly defined. Even acknowledging the difficulty of securing clear views from customers, too much customer research is on poorly focussed, broad topics that are too imprecise to support key decisions.

More sophisticated customer performance metrics do exist and are consequently closely monitored by Boards. Net Promoter Scores are one example of a common overall metric, and in some cases, these are tied to management incentive structures. However, as useful as overall barometers may be, they don't support the early identification of conformance problems nor are they designed to inform major strategic decisions. Material, specific problems associated with specific groups of customers can rarely be detected this way, including where business models or practices are at risk of exploiting vulnerable sections of the community.

By being deliberative on the expectations of the type of customer information they receive, chairs can ensure their Board has access to, for example:

- Direct exposure to outlier customer complaints data or even individual customer interactions. While they are outliers by nature, these can often provide generalised insights.
- Customer research that tests specific issues. Boards should take a warning signal when customer research is used as the primary justification for otherwise marginal investment cases – particularly where a research agency's underlying data has not been independently examined. But using well-designed customer research to support important business strategies enables Boards to make better decisions on key matters before them.
- Data on directly observed customer behaviour. Particularly for strategic choices that are said to respond to customer needs, Boards can and should request evidence of this in patterns of observed behaviour in current observations.

Boards obviously do not, and should not, see the amount of customer research that is needed to run a business day-to-day or even year-to-year. But equally, the idea that general purpose customer research can be repurposed to support the Board on critical decisions is misguided.

Why should the chair be focussed on information quality?

The idea that the chair should take considerable pains to improve the quality of information to support the workings of their Board is perhaps controversial. But if not the chair then who should take on this role? It should not be left to management, and while individual directors can express views there still seems a clear role for the chair to set and ensure standards are met.

In the battle between the right information and informational overload, much of the focus of the chair seems to have moved to volume control as a proxy for quality control. Obviously the ultimate goal must be for quality. Equally, quality needs to be cognisant of the types of information being considered. This is not an argument for more information, rather a clear call for raising the bar on the quality of information available to inform directors as they work to execute the increasingly difficult responsibilities before them.

No single recipe will give the Board the information they need to make every decision straightforward, or every governance problem easy to detect and remediate. Likewise, every suggestion made for greater diversity of Board constitution and information sources is, at one level, a more-of-the-same problem.

Having a well-structured agenda alone is unlikely to be enough to ensure the right volume and type of information. Even so, chairs with a well-developed sense of a Board's focus areas have the beginnings of a framework to curate higher quality information. Chairs can recognise and discuss the practical limits of a Board's ability to absorb information, not just in simplistic page limits but in the balance of preparation time required. Brutalist "one in, one out" rules on the number and/or length of Board papers can help force high-grading decisions, although this rule is typically broken the first time a complex matter comes before the Board.[71]

A nose for trouble

Our interviews around the leadership of the chair often returned to a concept that might be called a "nose for trouble". Earned through experience, this nose helps detect when information is too filtered, when decisions are too forced, or even when debate at the Board needs to continue to run.

What are these signs? Most of the directors we spoke to had some practical rules-of-thumb. Earned through experience, on the surface many appeared close to clichés or homespun truths, but on more careful consideration are nonetheless effective and, reflecting on our own experiences, many resonated with us.

Some of these included:

- Unexplained outperformance, or outperformance associated with a single overriding factor. Businesses can be lucky, but many directors sought to understand outperformance of this type to separate luck or unrepeatable factors from underlying and potentially worsening core performance.
- Requests for information that are not met or – more commonly – not met in a way that meets expectations. This would include information that is too complex to be understood, or not relevant to key issues. It also includes arguments based on personal credibility.
- Patterns of personal communication that indicate concerns about personal qualities. One director nominated excessive use of 'I' as an indication that a CEO should be watched for perhaps latent or masked narcissistic behaviour.
- Unexplained and rapid departures of key people, particularly

from the finance, HR or risk areas of the business.

- Unwillingness of departing executives and directors to participate fully in exit interviews.
- Unexplained changes in CEO behaviour, or in their support for key projects or initiatives. These changes can suggest that underlying business circumstances have shifted, perhaps in a way that hasn't yet appeared in reported results.
- Finally, 'hockey sticks' of all kinds, reflecting an unexplained improvement in performance after many years of decline.

Directors, but especially chairs, often have not only the experience of management, but also a level of distance that can enable them to help senior managers pick up early signs of real problems. This idea of a nose can at one level sound like a generalised catch all, but it's our contention that this is also a skill that can be learned and honed, if considered as a distinct contribution one can bring to the governance task.

Setting the pace and ambition of change

While a nose for trouble helps prevent or lessen the impact of missteps, chairs can equally have a critical role in achieving the goal of excellent company performance.

Many chairs recognise the challenge of managing the proportion of time devoted to compliance as well as performance. Even with the best information and experience around the Board table, allowing attention to overly focus on compliance can only bring a firm so far. At the end of the day, business performance is achieved by accepting and managing, not avoiding, risk.

That said, we would suggest that ensuring a sufficient proportion of time and effort is allocated to discussing performance is not enough to deliver superb performance.

In the private company space – like the private equity governance model we describe above – many firms benefit from leaders who may not have the title of chair but who act to set a performance agenda. Senior private equity fund partners or managing partners, for example, influence not only target returns of investee companies or overall funds, but also that investee firms are "pushing the envelope" or performing in a way that delivers value at the right combination of size and pace.

We've also observed in the public company sphere some chairs seek to have similar conversations with their Board colleagues and management. These conversations are framed not in terms of performance matching hurdles, or peer groups, although this can be an important first step. Almost by definition, leading companies surpass direct competitors and – to remain leading firms – must find new benchmarks or indicators of acceptable performance.

Chairs can and should drive these types of conversations. It should be the chair's job to ensure that the Board is constructively dissatisfied with current firm performance.

This chapter has set out to explore what we have come to view as a critical and yet largely under-explored area of governance – the leadership role of the chair. This is not to be critical of chairs, but rather to elevate the importance of the difficult role they inherit.

Commensurate with this is the recognition that performing the chair's role comes with a requirement that an appropriate amount of time be allocated to the task and, ipso facto, appropriate compensation. Some (non-chair) interviewees argued that in a major public company, the job of chair is near full-time, or at least three days per week in normal times. The implication of this is that a chair can only chair one major company, and probably not be a director of any other major company. We suspect many chairs would perhaps challenge this view, but believe it is consistent with the importance of the chair's leadership role as described there.

While beyond what we have examined here, if the above is true then it is to be expected that the chair's remuneration is way out of line with the CEO's. If paid more, chairs would have no financial reason to seek other Board roles, arguably increasing the quality of governance with, in broad terms, little overall increase in governance costs.

Concluding thoughts

Reasonable expectations of governance structure and processes

Public companies have been and should remain an important engine room for wealth creation, capital formation and innovation in advanced economies. Because of their sheer scale and importance, the ultimate governing body of each company, its Board, carries enormous responsibilities.

To say Boards are under more scrutiny and performance pressure than ever before would be an understatement. However, this is as it should be, for an obligation of any professional is to continue to improve their performance. This is especially the case when decisions before the Board are among the most important to a firm's success.

Equally, however, when one considers the complexity of issues before the typical large public company, and the increasing speed at which innovation is occurring, it is almost impossible to believe that rigid uniformity in terms of governance practices is an optimal approach. And yet that is what we observe: by and large unproven best practices set out what should at best be helpful guidelines but rapidly evolve to become uniform de facto rules. Ironically, the net effect of their ineffectiveness – and the consequent preference of employees and investors alike for superior models – may be to reduce the strength of the public company sector, disadvantaging some of the same stakeholders – smaller shareholders of all kinds – they are designed to protect.

Directors need, and indeed deserve, more than more-of-the-same responses to help them drive the performance of the companies they govern. Simultaneously they must meet explicit legal and implicit ethical obligations while achieving optimum outcomes. Theirs is not a simple task and more-of-the-same approaches do not help make these tasks more achievable.

Freedom to adapt is missing from the governance conversation. On balance the direction of travel is towards less agility in the ways Boards govern. As a result there is a greater mismatch between what Boards are focussed on, the make-up of the Boards, and the ingredients for success on the questions above. The different circumstances firms face mean this missing element will continue to make improved performance more difficult than it otherwise need be.

We contend there is a way out of the current governance trap. This entails Boards, with strong and effective leadership from the chair, designing and advocating the governance arrangements that best fit their particular company.

Many of the directors we spoke to feel that Boards are being held accountable for a range of unreasonable expectations. These might be unpicking deliberate concealment, being responsible for a bad investment when high quality processes are followed, or allowing their agenda to be unreasonably broadened.

Appealing to this type of reasoning is dodging the bullet. The right Boards with the right approaches can deal with these issues, and defend their actions when things don't work out has planned.

In fact, there is only one truly unreasonable expectation of Boards at present: it is that by simply carrying on doing more-of-the-same, they can improve the governance they are expected to provide.

APPENDICES

Appendix 1

Key findings of Strictly Boardroom

Strictly Boardroom deals with three questions about corporate governance.[72]

- What is the principal contemporary concern about the roles of the Board, directors, management and auditors?
- What are the key functions of a Board that require greater emphasis if this concern is to be addressed?
- To carry out these functions, what should be the responsibilities of directors and other parties involved in corporate governance and what other changes are needed in Board composition and processes?

The book answers these questions in the following way.

- Poor corporate performance, not fraud or misconduct, should be the main contemporary concern of corporate governance.
- Three factors in particular appear to contribute to many Boards' continuing acceptance of marginal corporate performance. These are:

  i. Confusion over board role and responsibilities, in particular a failure to balance the duty of the Board to ensure high levels of performance with its duties to oversee conformance by management with an increasing body of rules and regulations.

ii. Weak director selection processes.

iii. Lack of processes to keep performance at the centre of the Board's agenda.

To address this concern, the role and responsibilities of the Board should be clarified in the following terms:

- The key role of the Board should be to ensure that corporate management is continuously and effectively striving for above-average performance, taking account of risk. This is not to deny the Board's additional role with respect to shareholder protection. This role description is quite different to what is seen in other emerging statements such as "the Board's role is to ensure that no shareholder loses on their investment", or "the main role of the Board is to be society's policeman".

The essence of this statement is the requirement that the Board clearly define what is meant by sustainable, above-average performance, that its main monitoring should be with respect to performance so defined, and that it should act when it no longer has confidence that the management can deliver in these terms. This position does not equate performance with narrow, short-term measures such as quarterly earnings, but rather a more considered and longer-term set of measures developed by the Board.

This definition of the role of the Board leads to a new view of board functions that reflects the following three themes:

- Accentuate the Board's prime responsibility for setting

performance goals and monitoring management's progress in achieving those goals.
- De-emphasise the Board's role as a decision-making and initiating body. Instead the Board should require management to develop strategies, policies and proposals on major decisions.
- Place a greater emphasis on managerial accountability for formulating proposals for the Board and ensuring these proposals are implemented in practice.

This approach is not intended to diminish or weaken the role and responsibilities of the Board. The recommendations place a greater onus on the Board to act where it can and should have influence. It does this by forcing a Board to make hard decisions rather than taking the easier course of letting a marginally-performing management drift. At the same time, the Board must temper the pressure it places on management so that executives do not feel they need to commit illegal or unethical acts to "make target".

The Board's activities to enhance corporate performance could be improved by:

- More clearly defining the responsibilities of different types of directors, the Board chair, senior management and auditors.
- Board composition guidelines and operating procedures should be less concerned with numbers of directors by type (e.g. independent versus executive) and more concerned with the processes by which the non-executive directors work with each other, and with the Board as a whole, and with the quality and competence of each director.
- Using financial incentives to encourage the long-term performance orientation that the Board has agreed is most appropriate for its particular situation.

In respect of reform of the regulation of corporate governance, there is reason to treat sceptically claims that regulation will overcome collapses associated with 'boom/bust cycles'. There is also reason to be concerned that debate over legislative reform is a distraction from the more important improvement of firm performance. Finally, any new laws need to be assessed with sensitivity to their impact on shifting the attention of the Board from improving and sustaining performance to acting as a corporate policeman.

Appendix 2

ASX Corporate Governance Principles

1. Lay solid foundations for management and oversight: A listed entity should clearly delineate the respective roles and responsibilities of its Board and management and regularly review their performance.
2. Structure the Board to be effective and add value: The Board of a listed entity should be of an appropriate size and collectively have the skills, commitment and knowledge of the entity and the industry in which it operates, to enable it to discharge its duties effectively and to add value.
3. Instil a culture of acting lawfully, ethically and responsibly: A listed entity should instil and continually reinforce a culture across the organisation of acting lawfully, ethically and responsibly.
4. Safeguard the integrity of corporate reports: A listed entity should have appropriate processes to verify the integrity of its corporate reports.
5. Make timely and balanced disclosure: A listed entity should make timely and balanced disclosure of all matters concerning it that a reasonable person would expect to have a material effect on the price or value of its securities.

6. Respect the rights of security holders: A listed entity should provide its security holders with appropriate information and facilities to allow them to exercise their rights as security holders effectively.
7. Recognise and manage risk: A listed entity should establish a sound risk management framework and periodically review the effectiveness of that framework.
8. Remunerate fairly and responsibly: A listed entity should pay director remuneration sufficient to attract and retain high quality directors and design its executive remuneration to attract, retain and motivate high quality senior executives and to align their interests with the creation of value for security holders and with the entity's values and risk appetite.

Appendix 3

Davos Manifesto 2020: The Universal Purpose of a company in the Fourth Industrial Revolution

1. The purpose of a company is to engage all its stakeholders in shared and sustained value creation. In creating such value, a company serves not only its shareholders, but all its stakeholders – employees, customers, suppliers, local communities and society at large. The best way to understand and harmonise the divergent interests of all stakeholders is through a shared commitment to policies and decisions that strengthen the long-term prosperity of a company.

   i. A company serves its customers by providing a value proposition that best meets their needs. It accepts and supports fair competition and a level playing field. It has zero tolerance for corruption. It keeps the digital ecosystem in which it operates reliable and trustworthy. It makes customers fully aware of the functionality of its products and services, including adverse implications or negative externalities.

   ii. A company treats its people with dignity and respect. It honours diversity and strives for continuous improvements in working conditions and employee well-being. In a world of rapid change, a company fosters continued employability through ongoing upskilling and reskilling.

iii. A company considers its suppliers as true partners in value creation. It provides a fair chance to new market entrants. It integrates respect for human rights into the entire supply chain.

iv. A company serves society at large through its activities, supports the communities in which it works, and pays its fair share of taxes. It ensures the safe, ethical and efficient use of data. It acts as a steward of the environmental and material universe for future generations. It consciously protects our biosphere and champions a circular, shared and regenerative economy. It continuously expands the frontiers of knowledge, innovation and technology to improve people's well-being.

v. A company provides its shareholders with a return on investment that takes into account the incurred entrepreneurial risks and the need for continuous innovation and sustained investments. It responsibly manages near-term, medium-term and long-term value creation in pursuit of sustainable shareholder returns that do not sacrifice the future for the present.

2. A company is more than an economic unit generating wealth. It fulfils human and societal aspirations as part of the broader social system. Performance must be measured not only on the return to shareholders, but also on how it achieves its environmental, social and good governance objectives. Executive remuneration should reflect stakeholder responsibility.

3. A company that has a multinational scope of activities not only serves all those stakeholders who are directly engaged but acts itself as a stakeholder – together with governments and civil society – of our global future. Corporate global citizenship requires a company to harness its core competencies, its entrepreneurship, skills and relevant resources in collaborative efforts with other companies and stakeholders to improve the state of the world.

Endnotes

1 'Criminal Director liability: A bridge now too far?', John HC Colvin and Brendan Hord, Australian Journal of Corporate Law, Vol 35, 2020

2 Frederick G. Hilmer, *Strictly Boardroom: Improving Governance to Enhance Company Performance*, BRW Business Library, 2nd Edition, 1998, p 5

3 A summary of *Strictly Boardroom*'s findings and proposals are listed in Appendix 1.

4 Graham Bradley AM; *Is the Contemporary Corporation fit for purpose?*, lecture to the NSW Bar Association, March 2019

5 "Federal Reserve Shackles Wells Fargo After Fraud Scandal," *New York Times*, February 2 2018

6 "The Price of Wells Fargo's Fake Account Scandal Grows by $3 Billion," *New York Times*, February 21 2020

7 The Committee on the Financial Aspects of Corporate Governance, *Financial Aspects of Corporate Governance*, Final Report, December 1992

8 Kenneth Hayne, *Final Report*, Royal Commission into Misconduct in the Banking, Superannuation and Financial Services Industry, February 2019

9 Jillian Broadbent, John Laker and Graeme Samuel, *Final Report*, Prudential Inquiry into the Commonwealth Bank of Australia, May 2018

10 Graeme Samuel, Diane Smith-Gander and Grant Spencer, *Final Report*, Capability Review of the Australian Prudential Regulation Authority, June 2019

11 "Research Note – Report of the Royal Commission into HIH Insurance," Department of the Parliamentary Library, 13 May 2003

12 Kenneth Hayne, *Final Report*, Royal Commission into Misconduct in the Banking, Superannuation and Financial Services Industry, February 2019, Volume 1, Section 1.5.1, pp 8 - 9

13 Kate Towey and Charles Ashton, *COVID-19: Director Priorities for NFP recovery plans,* AICD website

14 W Richard Scott, *Organizations: rational, natural and open systems*, Prentice-Hall, 1981, p 114

15 Henry Louis Mencken, *Prejudices: Second Series*, Volume 2, Alfred A. Knopf, 1920, p 158

16 David Larcker and Brian Tayan, *Corporate Governance Matters*, Second Edition, p 7

17 Adolf A. Berle Jr and Gardiner C. Means, *The Modern Corporation and Private Property*, First Edition, p 18

18 This would include, for example, an executive negotiating on behalf of a firm supply arrangements with a company owned by themselves.

19 Many directors (including many directors we spoke to) and particularly chairs, spend much more than a day a month on their Board duties, or even on a single Board role. Even for these directors, a significant mismatch in time and focus remains.

20 David Beatty, *Shareholder Activism: This Changes Everything!*, Rotman Management, Winter 2017, p 7

21 Jim Collins and Jerry I. Porras, *Built to Last: Successful Habits of Visionary Companies*, Harper Business, 2002, p 91

22 Jillian Broadbent, John Laker and Graeme Samuel, *Final Report*, Prudential Inquiry into the Commonwealth Bank of Australia, May 2018, p4 . The panel found "a widespread sense of complacency has run through CBA, from the top down. CBA's first ranking on many financial measures created a collective belief within the institutions that CBA was well run and inherently conservative on risk, and this bred over-confidence, lack of appreciation for non-financial risks, and a focus on process rather than outcomes."

23 Frederick G. Hilmer, *Strictly Boardroom: Improving Governance to Enhance Company Performance*, BRW Business Library, 2nd Edition, 1998, p 4

24 This is a common metric, sometimes known as "economic value added".

25 Meghana Ayyagaru, Asli Demirguc-Kunt and Vojislav Maksimovic, "Who are America's Star Firms?", World Bank Policy Research Working Paper 8534, July 2018

26 Part of this difference can be explained by artefacts of accounting standards including, principally, the treatment of intangible assets and the different role of this type of asset between firms. We suspect this is scant comfort to investors.

27 ACCC, *Restoring electricity affordability and Australia's competitive advantage*, Retail Electricity Pricing Inquiry-Final Report, June 2018

28 Productivity Commission, *Competition in the Australian Financial System*, Inquiry Report, 29 June 2018

29 Max H Bazerman and Michael D. Watkins, *Predictable Surprises*, Harvard Business School Press, 2004

30 Professor Watkins was at HBS when the book was written, although he is now at IMD.

31 John Stensholt, "Child-care sums make listings look simple," *Business Review Weekly,* 10-16 October 2002, p 36

32 Australian Senate Education, Employment and Workplace Relationships References Committee, *Provision of childcare*, November 2009

33 Australian Senate Education, Employment and Workplace Relationships References Committee, *Provision of childcare*, November 2009, p 29

34 "ABC Learning Centres to be bought by Children 21", news.com.au, September 29 2009

35 ABC Learning, Inquiry Submission 86, p 2

36 The We Company, SEC Form S-1, August 2019, p8

37 The We Company, SEC Form S-1, August 2019, p 7

38 Joshua Franklin and Anirban Sen, "We Work delays IPO after frosty investor response," *Reuters Business News*, September 17 2019

39 Andrew Edgecliffe-Johnson, Eric Platt, Kana Inagaki and Judith Evans, "WeWork rescue: the winners and the losers", *Financial Times*, October 23 2019

40 George Hammond, "WeWork loses $2.1 billion and sheds members as lockdowns bite", *Financial Times*, May 21 2021

41 George Hammond, Arash Masoudi, Eric Platt and Andrew Edgecliffe-Johnson, "WeWork tells investors it lost $3.2 billion last year as it woos them for Spac deal", *Financial Times*, March 23, 2021

42 Author, *Predictable Surprises: The Disasters you Should Have Seen Coming, and How to Prevent Them*, Harvard Business Review Press, Michael D. Watkins, Max H. Bazerman, 2008

43 "Fees for no service" case studies are examined in Sections 1.2.1, 1.3.2, 2.2.1 and 2.3.2 of Volume 2 of the Final Report

44 Kenneth Hayne, *Final Report*, Royal Commission into Misconduct in the Banking, Superannuation and Financial Services Industry, February 2019, Sections 2.2.1 and 2.2.2 of Volume 2

45 Kenneth Hayne, *Final Report*, Royal Commission into Misconduct in the Banking, Superannuation and Financial Services Industry, February 2019, Section 3.2 of Volume 2

46 Kenneth Hayne, *Final Report*, Royal Commission into Misconduct in the Banking, Superannuation and Financial Services Industry, February 2019Section 3.2.3

47 Kenneth Hayne, *Final Report*, Royal Commission into Misconduct in the Banking, Superannuation and Financial Services Industry, February 2019, p 1- 4

48 'AGL ordered to pay $1.5 million for illegal door-to-door sales practices', ACCC Media Release 104/13

49 'EnergyAustralia ordered by consent to pay $1.2 million for unlawful sales tactics', ACCC Media Release MR 77/14

50 'Australian Power and Gas ordered by consent to pay $1.1 million for door to door sales conduct', ACCC Media Release 263/13

51 '$1 million in penalties for door-to-door sales', ACCC Media Release NR 207/12

52 'Origin to pay $2 million for unlawful door-to-door sales tactics', ACCC Media Release MR 45/15

53 Thomas Gryta and Ted Mann, "GE Powered the American Century – Then it Burned Out", *Wall Street Journal*, December 14, 2018

54 ASX Corporate Governance Council, *Corporate Governance Principles and Recommendations,* 4th Edition, February 2019, p2

55 Sally Linwood and Christian Gergis, "Changes to the latest ASX Corporate Governance Principles and Recommendations," *Company Director Magazine*, 1 April 2019

56 Graham Bradley, "Is the Contemporary Corporation Fit for Purpose?" NSW Bar Association Bathurst Lecture 2019

57 David Larcker and Brian Tayan, *Corporate Governance Matters*, Second Edition, p9

58 Larcker and Tayan identify these as: The Greenbury Report (1995) on executive compensation; the Hampel Report (1998) on the effectiveness of the Cadbury and Greenbury reports; the Turnbull Report (1999) on ways to improve corporate internal controls; the Higgs Report (2003) on the role, quality and effectiveness of non-executive directors; the Walker Review (2009) on corporate governance among UK banks; and 'Guidance on Board Effectiveness' by the Institute of Chartered Secretaries and Administrators (2011) which reviewed the Higgs report and recommended the withdrawal of many of its recommendations.

59 Submission to the Financial Reporting Council's enquiry on Proposed Revisions to the UK Corporate Governance Code, 2 March 2018

60 NYSE: Corporate Governance Guide, 2014, p 8

61 Eric Jackson, "Why Narcissistic CEOs Kill Their Companies," *Forbes*, January 11, 2012

62 Warren Bennis and James O'Toole, "Don't Hire the Wrong CEO", *HBR*, May-June 2000

63 www.roberthalf.com.au/research-insights/ceo-tracker

64 Harvard Law School Governance Forum; posted by Dan Marcec February 12 2018. https://corpgov.law.harvard.edu/2018/02/12/ceo-tenure-rates/

65 Corrs Chambers Westgarth, "The role of the Chair: insights from ASIC v Mitchell (No 2)", 23 September 2020

66 Stansilav Shekshnia, "How to be a good board chair", *Harvard Business Review,* March-April 2018

67 'Many are called, few are chosen – an analysis of the composition of ASX300 boards from 2005 – 2020' Ownership Matters, October 2020

68 One possible implication of this is that many investors believe management is much more informed about business performance than Board members.

69 David R. Beatty, "How activist investors are transforming the role of public-company boards," in *The Board Perspective: A collection of McKinsey insights focusing on boards of directors*, March 2018

70 Less helpfully for the authors, Beatty also suggests that "instead of having to spend millions on a consulting review, you could get one for free from would-be activist investors".

71 This type of rule is particularly unworkable when it is linked to

demands for "only slides", a specification that coupled with a page limit seriously degrades the quality of thought it is possible to include in a compliant paper.

72 Frederick G. Hilmer, *Strictly Boardroom: Improving Governance to Enhance Company Performance*, BRW Business Library, 2nd Edition, 1998, pp 2–7

INDEX